THE LIFE BEYOND DEATH

THE LIFE
BEYOND DEATH

by Arthur Ford
as told to Jerome Ellison

W. H. ALLEN
A division of Howard and Wyndham Ltd
1972

Printed in Great Britain by
Fletcher & Son Ltd, Norwich
for the publishers W. H. Allen and Co Ltd,
43 Essex Street, London WC2R 3JG
Bound by Richard Clay (The Chaucer Press) Ltd
Bungay, Suffolk

ISBN 0 491 00933 X

ACKNOWLEDGMENTS

I know that Arthur Ford would want to acknowledge, as I most certainly do, the generous contributions of the Reverend Canon William V. Rauscher, a council member and former president of Spiritual Frontiers Fellowship, to the conception and completion of this book. He would want to thank, as I do, Susan Graham, his cousin Ellis Ford, and my wife, Miriam Ellison, all of whom, each in his way, contributed to making this book. I am also grateful for the grant of sabbatical freedom generously provided by the board of governors of the University of New Haven.

J. E.

Contents

MY FRIEND ARTHUR FORD:
An Introduction

My Friend Arthur Ford:
An Introduction

"EIGHTY PERCENT of the questions people ask me during the question periods after my lectures," Arthur Ford said to me one day early in 1970—he was then in his seventy-fourth year and had behind him more than four decades as one of the world's most famous trance mediums—"have to do with the nature of life after death. What kind of body do we have? Can we remember all the things that happened during our earth life? Will we remember all the people we knew? What will be our relationship with these people? With various historical figures long since passed on? With—if we are religiously inclined—the great souls which figure so prominently in whatever religion we have adhered to? What are we supposed to do over there? Do we just loaf, or do we have specific duties? Where does God figure in this? Will we meet him right away, or must we go through a period of probation? Is there anything to this notion of having to go through a period of torment, or is life in the world beyond in general a pleasant place?

"There are definite answers to all these questions. They have been accumulating for centuries and, though generally neglected by a materialistically oriented world, are surprisingly unified in their general content.

"These questions are terribly important to millions and millions of people. Some of them are almost beside themselves with grief over the loss of some loved person. Some are themselves facing the end of their days here and are in great anxiety about what may be in store for them. I have always felt it was one of the most important parts of my job here to give these people a reassurance that comes from having straight answers to such questions.

"Now," he said, "here comes the pitch. I don't know how much time I'm going to have here." He had for a number of years suffered from an angina condition which had become increasingly serious. By far the most intuitive person I have ever met, he knew that anything he expected to accomplish on the "earth plane" would have to be dealt with fairly soon. "I want to do a book which will wrap up everything I know about life after death. Doing it alone is beyond my strength. Will you help?"

I had assisted Arthur Ford in the preparation of his previous book, *Unknown but Known*. He had been pleased with my editorial assistance and had graciously acknowledged it in the book's foreword. My entire experience with Arthur Ford had been a great adventure in learning; working with him in this way had greatly extended my understanding of the universe of which we all are a part. I said I'd be delighted to help in any way I could. We had various conferences and agreed on what the general content of the book was to be. The work was gathering momentum nicely when, on January 4, 1971, only a few days short of his seventy-fifth birthday, Arthur Ford died. There were conferences between me, the officers of that splendid nationwide organization Spiritual Frontiers Fellowship (which Arthur had helped found and in whose work he had always been a revered leader), the publishers, and the great medium's many friends on what should be done about the nearly completed book. The book you hold in your hand is the outcome of these meetings.

This gives only part of the story of how this book came to be written. To give the whole story would involve much more. It would have to mention, for example, the young New Jersey clergyman, who had also been a friend of Arthur Ford, who said to me, "Please finish the book as quickly as you can. We who work daily with the bereaved, the frightened, and the desperately depressed have immediate need of something to place in their hands that will help them see some of the deeper dimensions of eternity as Arthur did when he was with us." It would have to tell—even if only in the form of a brief synopsis—a little bit of the remarkable story of how a young college student and World War I draftee—through a fantastic series of mysteries, accidents, and coincidences—became a world figure who shares with Edgar Cayce the distinction of being one of the two truly great American mediums of the twentieth century. I would even have to tell enough about myself to make clear how I came to meet Arthur Ford, how we became friends and, finally, collaborators.

"Everybody," Arthur Ford assured us many times, "has psychic ability, just as everybody has the ability to strike the keys of a piano keyboard. But, of course, not everybody develops these abilities to the level of becoming a concert pianist."

Psychically, I have come to think of myself as a kind of American "Mr. Average." As a small boy in Sunday school, I loved the stories of the New Testament miracles just as any child loves tales that are seemingly magical. My birthday is near Halloween and was always celebrated with the Halloween symbols—jack-o'-lanterns, strange sounds and shapes in the dark, and genial spooks. When I was nine years old, my mother lay in a coma for a while, near death, after a hemorrhage during childbirth. After her recovery she told me of her experience—which much later I was to learn was fairly common—of "crossing over" to the beyond (which she described as a lovely place) and being sent back to finish her work here. Once, while lying in the grass on a summer day and looking at the sky, I had an altogether extraordinary experience of being let in on the secrets of the universe.

But boyhood daydreaming soon passed. In college I entered an extremely rigorous regimen of scientific study and became skeptical about anything that smacked of the mystical, the occult, or the otherworldly. However, something in me rebelled against the cut-and-dried materialism of science. Toward the end of my undergraduate studies I switched to the study of literature and after graduation I became a journalist. In this activity I prospered, and eventually was able to gratify one of my boyhood ambitions—to own and operate an airplane. One time, flying a plane which was not equipped with blind flying navigational instruments, I got lost in the clouds and could not find my way out. My plane could not climb above the cloud cover, so I could not go up. The cloud fog apparently went all the way to the dangerous tangle of hills, trees, chimneys, and power lines on the ground so I could not safely go down. I could not stay where I was without risking a deadly spin. I was trapped. Spontaneously, I prayed to be shown the way out of the trap. Clammy with fear, I put the nose of the plane down toward the dangers of the ground and held it there. Before long a white farmhouse emerged in the mist. I circled it and on the second circle cut low for a landing. Just before touching ground, I could see, under the bottom of the cloud cover, that the house was on a hill; beyond it in the valley, was clear, safe air. I was immediately reoriented and within ten minutes was safely on the ground at my home airport. Something or Somebody had heard me and taken me to safety, I was sure. After that I was never again quite so cocksure about a simple, cause-and-effect, fully material universe.

Other things happened. Free-lance writers have a certain advantage over other people: Very often they can help complete their education through their work. Simply to learn more about the subject, I wrote an article on extrasensory perception (ESP). While writing this piece I discovered that I had certain minor but also definite abilities in telekinesis, clairvoyance, and telepathy. Don't get me wrong; these gifts were not spectacular; I could not always demonstrate them, and when I could, the demonstration was weak. That they were *there* could not be questioned. I could develop them if I wanted to invest the necessary effort. For me, the old concept of a totally materialistic universe was permanently shattered.

There followed a stretch of my life which I have come to think of as my "Purgatorial Preview." During this period it seemed to me that everything that could go wrong in my life went wrong—sometimes annoyingly, sometimes disastrously, sometimes tragically. From serene and prosperous success I seemed suddenly plunged into personal, social, marital, financial, and professional failure and chaos. One of my flamboyant literary adventures failed with heavy financial loss. My then wife insisted upon a divorce; this brought about an abrupt severance of all my accustomed social, professional, and family ties. One night a few years after this I received a telephone call informing me that my only son, then sixteen, had been fatally injured. Since college days I had been an enthusiastic and convivial drinker. Later I began to use alcohol as a temporary escape from some of my perplexities. It only made them worse.

It was at this time that I recalled with a new meaning my experience in the airplane. Something or Somebody had once fetched me out of physical clouds and set me on physical solid ground. Might it not be possible that this same mysterious agent might steer me out of my present social and emotional vapors? I tried asking, and some remarkable things began to happen.

Employing the usual self-educating techniques of the free-lance writer, I wrote a couple of magazine pieces on the work of Alcoholics Anonymous. This not only brought me new and helpful understanding of my drinking, but was the occasion for my meeting one of the cofounders of AA, Bill, whom in the course of time I came to know quite well. (Bill, by established AA tradition, could be known only by his first name while he lived. Anonymity could be broken only after death. Bill died only a few weeks after Arthur's death. I am, therefore, now at liberty to refer to this former Wall Street broker and co-founder of Alcoholics Anonymous by his full and proper name, William G. Wilson.)

During one of our long and excited talks (both of us loved to gab about the problems of man and the general nature of things, particularly things still only partly understood and therefore mysterious) I mentioned to him my investigations into ESP and my interest in the occult. I told him about my reading in the findings of the British Society for Pyschical Research, the reports of the inner experiences of the swamis, and the writings of the great Swiss psychiatrist C. G. Jung. Unexpectedly, I found in Bill a staunch and helpful guide into this new realm. Dr. Jung, it turned out, had unwittingly, through the truth he implanted in the mind of one of his alcoholic patients and which this patient had passed on to others, been one of the influences which culminated in the founding of AA. Bill himself had had a number of experiences of a very nonmaterialistic sort, and he told me about them. Then, unexpectedly, he said: "If you're really interested in this stuff, you should get to know Art Ford."

I had read about the great medium but had really never expected to have the luck to meet him, much less "get to know" him. "He's one of us, you know," Bill said. (Tradition requires that the identity of an AA member cannot be revealed except by the express act of the member himself. Since Arthur has told of his membership in one of his books, I am permitted to mention it here.) One of Ford's public lectures was scheduled for our part of the world at about this time, and I arranged to attend.

Ford's appearance surprised (I almost wrote "shocked") me. I had expected that one of the world's truly great trance mediums would have at least a little something of the spooky about him. There was nothing frail, ethereal, or otherworldly about the way Arthur came on. When in a happy mood, as he always was during his public appearances (I was later to learn that he could have other moods, too!), he was a plump, round-faced, jovial man, quick of mind and of wit, always on the edge of cracking a friendly joke with his characteristic shy smile and twinkle of eye. During the "readings" (messages from departed spirits to members of the audience) I was one of several in the audience who received stunningly veridical communications. After the lecture I was introduced to Ford. We fell to talking about our mutual friend Bill and discovered an immediate liking for each other—a liking which never diminished to the time of Arthur's death. From then on I was fortunate enough to be one of a small group of persons privileged to participate in some séances Arthur gave out of his great overflowing friendliness "just for the fun of it."

What about this strange man whom I had just met and who was to become such a firm friend? My curiosity had never run at a higher pitch. I crammed my head full of information about him (and, as you might by now suspect, eventually did a magazine article about him).

Arthur Ford was born in the little Florida town of Titusville, which, at the time of his birth—1896—had a population of about 300. His father, a steamboat captain, was "one of those ardent nonchurchgoing Episcopalians." Not long after Arthur's birth the family moved to Fort Pierce, Florida, where his "*very* Baptist" mother soon became active in the church of her persuasion. Arthur spent his boyhood in Fort Pierce, and, as he tells the story, a great part of his life centered on the Fort Pierce Baptist church. Arthur was playing the piano at the young people's meetings—where hymn singing was an important part of every program—when he was twelve years old. Right from the time when he was first able to think seriously about such matters, the boy's interest in religion was intense. So constant was his devotion to the Baptist Church that it was pretty well understood that he would eventually go into the ministry, and that it would be the *Baptist* ministry.

Arthur, however, now began to show that streak of independent theological thinking that was to be one of his distinguishing characteristics all his life. He met some Unitarians, attended some of their meetings, and was deeply impressed by their doctrine. After exposure to the comparative intellectual freedom of Unitarianism, the Baptist faith as propounded in Fort Pierce at that time seemed narrow and stuffy. Arthur threw so many embarrassing questions at the leaders of the Baptist Church that, when he was sixteen years old, they found it necessary to throw him out on grounds that his faith had become "corrupted." The Unitarians, as it happened, did not capture him. When he left Fort Pierce to become a student at Transylvania University in Lexington, Kentucky, he was a member of the Christian Church (Disciples of Christ) , in which he was eventually to become an ordained minister.

One time I asked Ford when he first became aware that he possessed unusual psychic powers. The question seemed to puzzle him. "As a boy, I always seemed to know pretty much what other people were thinking," he told me. "How was I to know there was anything very special about *that*? I just assumed everybody had telepathic pickup. It wasn't until I got into the Army that I discovered I was a little different in this respect from the general run of people."

Ford was a draftee in 1917 and was sent to Camp Grant. The next year the Great Flue Epidemic of 1918 raged through the country, striking the Camp Grant soldiers with special fury. While Ford was there, several soldiers were dying of influenza every night. One night he dreamed that a sheet of paper was handed him; on it was written in large and clearly legible letters the names of the soldiers who had died in the camp during the night. On getting up, he told his buddies in the barracks of his dream. After breakfast the daily camp bulletin came out; the list was exactly the same as the one Ford had dreamed! For some days this continued. Each night he dreamed the names of those who had died, and each morning his list was verified. His fellow soldiers began to shun him as a harbinger of death. He soon learned not to talk about his dreams but was deeply troubled by them.

Ford was honorably discharged from the Army and returned to Transylvania in 1919. Once back on the campus, he sought the help of a professor of psychology who, over the years, had earned the reputation of being unusually sympathetic and understanding—Dr. Elmer Snoddy. In Snoddy's kindly company, young Ford spilled the whole story of his spontaneous psychic experiences, which by this time were becoming both more numerous and more vivid. There were not only the Camp Grant episodes, but many others. There was the time he saw the face of his brother George vividly before him at the exact moment when, he later learned, George was dying of complications following influenza. There were the college-dormitory experiments in table tilting; the table took on extraordinary powers of communication when Arthur was participating. There was the incident of Joe, one of his fraternity brothers who had joined in the table tilting. When Joe was on his deathbed with pneumonia, he called Arthur to him and gave him a code word. "If this should come through to you," Joe said, "you will know it's me." Joe died. A year later, Arthur got the code word while sitting in a séance with another medium.

"What did all this mean?" Arthur wanted to know. Was he somehow mentally deranged, and if so, how could he ever be straightened out? The friendly and learned Snoddy told him what he knew about psychic phenomena. There were times, he said, when information entered the human mind by means still not thoroughly understood. He told the eagerly listening young Ford of the studies then in progress aimed at a better understanding of these events. The great Harvard philosopher-psychologist Dr. William James had become deeply interested in such studies and was encouraging methodical scientific study of these phenomena. In England, under the aegis of the British Society for Psychical Research and such great pioneers as Sir Oliver Lodge, Henry Sidgwick, and Frederic Myers, such studies were far advanced. Among these scholars, Snoddy said, the matter would be simple and clear-cut. Ford was one of those rare people, a medium; there was no reason why he should not accept his gifts, develop them, and use them in the service of mankind. Greatly reassured, Arthur went back to his studies—and to his psychical work, gradually learning to control his abilities in an orderly way for public demonstration.

From here on, Ford quickly became adjusted to his new role as a practicing medium. Many people who were able and willing to help him came his way; he actively sought out many others. In 1921 he went to New York to see Miss Gertrude Tubby, secretary of the American Society for Psychical Research. Miss Tubby arranged for him to meet Dr. Franklin Prince and to have sittings with some of the most reliable mediums in the great city. In 1922 he was married, ordained a Christian minister, and appointed pastor of a church in Barbourville, Kentucky. During a very successful two years as minister, he continued to attend séances and applied himself diligently to his continued development as a medium.

While in Barbourville, Ford was visited by Dr. Paul Pearson, who directed very extensive Chautauqua circuits throughout the East. Pearson, it developed, was intensely interested in psychic phenomena and had been personally acquainted with such great scholars in this field as Sir Oliver Lodge and Sir Arthur Conan Doyle. He wanted Ford to give a series of lectures on psychic matters in New England during the summer of 1924. Ford accepted. It was the beginning of his career as a world-renowned platform personality—and it was the end of his marriage. The young Mrs. Ford, a Kentucky girl with strong attachments to her girlhood family, would not go north with him. Arthur, a great success on the lecture circuit, was invited to stay on for the winter lecture series. He was now on his way. His bride never came north, he never returned to Kentucky, and in the

course of time they were amiably and somewhat perfunc-
torily divorced.

Arthur now began to meet, and become personally
acquainted with, some of the great figures in that realm
of investigation into the nature of the human psyche
which is now called parapsychology. The inspiration and
counsel of these able and experienced men and women
helped him give shape and expression to his drive to comprehend more fully the nature of the world beyond death
—the same drive which, almost half a century later, was
to culminate in the publication of this book. One of these
men was the celebrated Far Eastern swami Paramahansa
Yogananda, author of that famous classic in its field *Autobiography of a Yogi* and one of the great influences in
broadening and deepening understanding between
Eastern and Western religious concepts. Yogananda himself was, of course, a highly accomplished psychic. While
fully appreciating Arthur's psychic gifts, he attached less
importance to these manifestations than to the development of nobility of spirit and of soul. Arthur never became a disciple of yoga in the usual sense. He did become
a friend of Yogananda. The great swami (as Arthur Ford
will relate in his own words in a later chapter of this
book) had clear ideas about the nature of the world beyond based on visionary revelations he regarded as utterly dependable. As Ford's own experience broadened,
he found more and more corroboration of Yogananda's
insights.

Arthur Ford's public appearances featured a straightforward lecture on psychic phenomena followed by a
"message period," during which he would stand before
his audience and deliver to people who were present

what purported to be identifying messages from friends
and relatives who had died. Much of Ford's world reputation was based on the quality of these messages. There
are many thousands of people (among them myself) who
will testify that these messages contained identifying information that could not possibly have been prearranged
and could not possibly have originated with anyone but
the now-discarnate individual who claimed to be the
sender. I had always been curious about Ford's exact
state of mind at the times these messages were "coming
through" and asked him about it. Apparently it was as
though he could use his mind as a kind of frequency-
tuning device to tune in on various wavelengths of
existing reality. When the everyday world was
in sharp focus, the world of discarnates was blurred or
nonexistent to his consciousness. When he turned some
hidden mental knob to bring him more sharply the
thoughts and presence of discarnate beings, the everyday
world became blurred.

It should be noted here that Arthur Ford's fame rested
upon the fact that he was the world's most effective
"mental" medium. The qualifying adjective "mental" is
used to distinguish those who bring messages from another sphere of existence from those who produce physical phenomena—voices, lights, movement of tables,
chairs and objects, levitations, and so on. The greatest of
the physical mediums was D. D. Home, a nineteenth-
century American whose demonstrations of telekinesis
(movement of physical objects by mental means) aston-
ished qualified observers in the cultural centers of
America and Europe. Ford's achievement was to produce
the greatest body of recorded veridical evidence of

human survival after death ever contributed to psychical research by any one medium. It will be rewarding, I think, in terms of a fuller understanding of some of the later chapters in this book, to nail down Ford's "tuning-in" process. The following is his own description of this state of mind as given in his story of his life:

I accepted an invitation to lecture for a time in the First Spiritualist Church of New York City which met on Sunday evenings in Carnegie Hall. I was fortunate in that this was a critical audience, accustomed to hearing more distinguished men than I and to seeing excellent demonstrations of psychic gifts. So I had to extend myself and work at my own development. At that time, before I had finished my studies with Swami Yogananda, my mediumship was still somewhat sporadic and I never knew whether I would get results or not. When strangers wanted to reach their departed relatives through me, I was willing to be the go-between, but sometimes no relatives appeared! How was I to know whether the relatives refused to communicate with their earth-bound family or whether I was not properly geared for transmission? In other words, was the line down, or was there just no one at its other end? Usually, however, in a public meeting some of those persons in the audience had relatives ready to converse.

I found that my main task on such occasions was to make myself open to whatever might come through. Soon the result was a fairly consistent ability to stand before an audience, half block out the people before me, feel as if I were about to go into trance but not lose consciousness, and then let discarnate personalities either appear before me or impress me with a description of themselves while at the same time I heard, wordlessly, the messages they wished to convey.

Whenever I threw my critical mind into a skeptical mood, telling myself, "This man couldn't be named Gregory Klegory Tegory," and tried to substitute something which sounded more sensible, then I misfired. But when I went ahead and reported what I heard or saw, the result was usually a response from someone in the audience.

Although I was doing a fair amount of public work, I thought of myself as an amateur and fully intended to go into some other profession as soon as I learned a little more about the reach of the mind. I remember the day I realized that my own psychic powers no longer seemed strange. If I had been looking for an analogy I suppose I would have said that now I felt like a horse with its blinders off. I was less hedged in. The universe had widened. Most of all, life made more sense, for apparently death did not put an end to man's strivings nor to his concern for his loved ones.

As my public work increased I used to wish there were some way to hold back the crowds of discarnates who pressed about me. Sometimes I "saw" them, sometimes I felt them, but either way there were often too many of them. There should be some method, or someone, to keep them in order, to determine precedence. I had to take whoever clamored the loudest, silent though the clamor might be. What was needed was an invisible master of ceremonies. It was at this point that a partner came into my life and Fletcher became my right-hand man.

Most mediums, in their professional work, are closely associated with a discarnate personality called a control—

a kind of psychic master of ceremonies who takes over the medium's vocal apparatus and takes charge of proceedings during trance séances while the medium himself is entranced and, to all appearances, asleep. During the early years of his mediumship, Arthur Ford worked without a control. Then, suddenly, in 1924, a personality broke into one of Ford's séances and, using the sleeping Ford's voice box, said, "When Ford wakes up, tell him that from now on I will be his control and that I go by the name of Fletcher." Naturally curious about the identity of his new discarnate associate, Ford asked sitters at later séances to find out all they could. Fletcher generously supplied information, established himself as a person in his own right, and eventually became as much of a friend to habitual sitters at Ford séances as was Arthur himself.

Fletcher gave his family name and full details about his life and death. For reasons of his own, Arthur never publicized the family name of his control. This tradition will of course be respected here, but we are at liberty to publish Fletcher's biography in considerable detail. During Arthur's boyhood, there had been a small colony of French Canadians living across the river from where the Fords lived. One of the reasons for withholding Fletcher's last name came from Fletcher himself: His family were staunch Roman Catholics. They had fixed ideas about the nature of life after death which did not at all correspond to the facts as Fletcher had experienced and observed them; he did not want to embarrass them publicly with uncomfortable truth. Fletcher's family had left Fort Pierce and returned to Canada. Fletcher had enlisted in World War I and been killed in action. He gave numerous details about himself which Ford was later able to confirm: the military unit of which he was a member; the nature and place of his death; the members of his surviving family and their addresses. "Well, check it out," was a characteristic phrase used by Arthur Ford whenever somebody questioned some startling or unusual fact which came through in a séance. He often followed his own advice and did so in the case of Fletcher. In all details, Fletcher "checked out."

Since Arthur Ford's death, many have asked, "What will Fletcher do now? Will he become the control of some other medium? Will he 'close up shop'? What will he do?" Fletcher has given us the answer to these questions. His answers are given us by Arthur Ford in the later chapters of this book.

In 1926 Arthur Ford was for the first time catapulted into worldwide newspaper headlines. At that time the leading figure in international vaudeville circuits was a marvelously ingenious magician named Harry Weiss, who worked under the professional name Houdini. After the death of Houdini's mother, to whom he was deeply attached, the great magician sought sittings with numerous mediums. A transcendant expert in all forms of illusion, Houdini could easily detect the frauds among them. Deception in this area—a province so closely affecting the profoundest hopes of man—infuriated the magician. He barnstormed the country, sought séances with every medium he could find, ruthlessly exposed the frauds, and made lurid headlines whenever he did so. However, his investigations ended by having a sobering effect upon him. Some of the mediums he sat with could not be exposed: They were not frauds. Their messages were apparently what they purported to be—that is, direct communications from people presumed to be dead. This made Houdini thoughtful. Deciding to put the matter to the final test, he made an agreement with his wife, Beatrice, that the one to die first would attempt to communicate with the other, using a special, elaborate, previously agreed-upon code which would positively identify the sender beyond any possible question. Houdini died in 1926.

In 1927 Arthur Ford made his first lecture tour in England. His first introduction was to a very large audience in London and was made by Sir Arthur Conan Doyle. A fulsome account of the occasion, including high praise for Ford's performance from Doyle, appeared in the next morning's paper. Arthur Ford's reputation was now as solidly established in Europe as in America. He met and came to know the dignitaries of the British Society for Psychical Research, including Sir Oliver Lodge, and arranged sittings with the leading mediums of England. When he returned to America in 1928, he was more than ever in demand as a lecturer and had more requests for private sittings than he could possibly accommodate. It must now be established that Ford did not like Houdini; he regarded much of the magician's "exposing" as bigoted, flamboyant, and unfair. He was therefore much surprised, on awakening from trance after a sitting on February 8, 1928, to be told that he had delivered a message from Houdini's mother: the one word "forgive." During the séance Houdini's mother, speaking through Ford, explained that this was the message she and her son Harry had agreed upon, before her death, as the one that would positively identify her. Because of Ford's dislike for Houdini, he felt no need to do anything about the message. Others at the sitting, however, took it upon themselves to notify Mrs. Beatrice Houdini. Mrs. Houdini at once, and publicly, expressed her amazement and delight. It was the only one of thousands of purported messages that had been relayed to her that was correct. Harry's mother had failed to "get through" to him during his lifetime. Now that a channel had been opened, his mother said, Harry himself would be able to come through with the agreed-upon message to his wife.

The messages that followed during the ensuing weeks turned out to be one of the great classical communications in the annals of psychical research. It was unusually well attested. An editor of the *Scientific American* was present throughout all the sittings. He brought with him a shorthand expert who took down every word spoken. When the entire communication was finished, it was attested by Mrs. Houdini to be in actual fact the long, precisely worded communication, delivered in the complicated code which Houdini and his wife had used in their vaudeville act together, agreed upon before Houdini's death as his positive identification. This news made even bigger headlines than Houdini's original debunking campaign had. Arthur Ford's name was in the newspapers for many weeks. He was now world-famous.

The next twenty years of Ford's life contained dizzying extremes of triumph and disaster. On the one hand, his fame spread and his autobiography was published by a major publisher. At the other extreme, he was overtaken by an almost unbelievable sequence of personal catastrophes. For one thing, he developed the heart condition which—in January, 1971—finally killed him. Twice he was stricken with heart attacks when alone, and by "pure chance" help and resuscitation arrived in the nick of time. In 1930 he and his sister, who had also moved to New York, and a friend made a trip to Florida to visit their parents. On the way back their car was struck by a truck. His sister and the friend were killed. Ford, suffering from fractures, lacerations, and internal injuries, was in a hospital with little chance of recovery. During his convalescence he was given injudicious amounts of morphine by the attending physician. Months later he was recovered from his physical injuries—but made the horrifying discovery that he had become addicted to morphine. He put himself through the agonizing "cold turkey" separation and broke the habit. Afterward, however, he lived in a state of almost unbearable nervous tension. A friend suggested that he take a drink now and then to relieve it. Until then Ford had been a teetotaler. He tried alcohol and discovered he liked it. A few years later he found he liked it all too well. "I was going on some fairly substantial drunks," he told me later, a twinkle in his eyes. It was an understatement. He was now as in deep despair over alcohol as he had been over drugs. At this time Alcoholics Anonymous came to his rescue. He was everlastingly grateful. Thereafter, his framed and autographed photograph of Bill Wilson went with Arthur Ford wherever he traveled. It was the first item to be unpacked and was always displayed in a prominent place. At about this same time I, too, had come to know Bill. It was through Bill, as I have said, that Arthur and I first met.

During the twenty years of our earth-side friendship, I saw Arthur Ford in all his moods and in several places of residence. He visited me in Indiana during my professor-

ship there; at my summer place on Cape Cod; and at my
present home in Guilford, Connecticut. I visited him in
his New York apartment when he lived there; in his Philadelphia flat after he had moved to that city; and in his
house in Coral Gables, Florida. Once he accepted you as
friend, Arthur was unshakably devoted. Except when he
was in one of his black moods (I accepted his as he did
mine) he was a fascinating conversationalist and a de-
lightful companion. Our conversation ranged from out-
and-out good-humored nonsense, through the whole
range of ordinary chitchat, swapping jokes, and down-
right gossip, to abrupt plunges into all that was most
profound in the life of man, the cosmic intent of God,
and the structure of the universe.

Our friendship was full of strange crisscrosses. One of
them was our independent relationships with the late
Bishop James Pike. When Pike first began to attract public attention with his progressive ideas, I did a full-length
magazine profile on him. During the interviews I came
to know Pike quite well. I met his wife and the son who
later was to make such tragic world headlines. Four years
later Ford met Pike. Pike's son had committed suicide;
the bishop had become interested in psychic phenomena,
had obtained a sitting with Ford, and, through him, been
in direct touch with—so he affirmed—his "deceased" son.
Once again, the name of Arthur Ford was in newspaper
headlines around the world.

"In this new book," Arthur Ford told me early in the
planning stage of the present volume, "I don't want to
get into any evidential stuff at all. So far as I'm concerned, the evidence on human survival of death is

already in. People can look at it or not, they can believe it or not, but that part of the job is done—and well done.

"What I want to do now is take it from there, and go on to the matter of what it's actually *like* after we die. I want to talk about the experience itself—the quality, substance, content of life on these other planes."

As his amanuensis, I had my instructions. We went on from there until, on December 19, 1970, when Arthur Ford dated his last letter to me, all the planning, discussion, and research for the book had already been done, and a publisher's contract awaiting his signature was on his desk. All that remained now was for me to put his thoughts through the typewriter. His extraordinary last letter to me, which I will presently quote in length, contained what turned out to be his final instructions on this work. He died on January 4, 1971. Because I think it will add so much to the understanding and enjoyment of this book, because it will help define the special and limited area the book undertakes to illuminate, and because it will add something to the record of how this unique man went about his unprecedented work, I am here adding a few prefatory words about how we worked together.

Though unfailingly articulate and often brilliant on the lecture platform, to put anything down on paper seemed an agony for Arthur Ford. He avoided such labor altogether when he could, and when he couldn't, he would turn out rough copy for somebody else to edit and get into shape for publication. This job fell to me. It was a Jack-Sprat-and-wife situation. I enjoy writing and found the material fascinating. We hit it off.

That Arthur Ford read unceasingly and over a broad range during his entire life is an important fact in explaining the unusual quality of his mediumship. According to his own theory of discarnate communication via trance medium, the communicator must work with the vocabulary and intellectual stock-on-hand of the medium. If the communicator is attempting subtle, high-level, complex communication, he may be frustrated or his message distorted if the medium's stock-on-hand is sparse. That intelligible messages purporting to be from such a wide range of specialists—engineers, architects, scientists, physicians, surgeons, space technicians, opera singers, statesmen, and writers—have come through clearly stands as a tribute to Ford's erudition, as well as to the rare quality of his gift.

Ford read not only extensively, but creatively. He constantly compared what he read with his own experience and observation. If what he read did not match what he knew to be so, he simply discarded it. If it did, he filed it in his vast memory and referred to it again and again. A good part of my editorial work with him was handled through references to something he had read.

"Now in this particular matter," he would say, "I go along with Myers up to this point, but from here on I hold to somewhat different ideas." He would then outline his own view. He both needed and enjoyed the reinforcement of other minds and broke from stated precepts only when the urgency of his own experience obliged him to. One time, when we were working on *Unknown but Known*, I was trying to clarify an important point concerning his technique of meditation. He made one or two tries to get it across to me, and then almost in exasperation he exclaimed, "You've said it yourself! You've said it yourself!" He then quoted accurately something I

had written years before and had nearly forgotten. These
instances, which were many, indicate how Ford thought
of himself in relation to the total field of parapsychology.
He did not think of himself as an innovator. He labored
to make his contribution, such as it might be, in a field
already discovered and broadly mapped by others. As the
evidence of his own mediumship piled up around him,
he began to feel that his special contribution would be to
leave an unprecedented volume of evidential, verifiable
material indicating that those who die are not dead, but
live.

Those who knew him were filled with admiration of
the vigor, and sometimes appalled at the recklessness,
with which he gave himself to his task. A single-minded
sense of high purpose was one of the dominant characteristics of his life. Though his living quarters sometimes
gave a helter-skelter impression, and though he was a
harum-scarum dasher about the country and the world,
there was never a time when these dashings about were
not motivated by some high purpose. At first, it was a
simple realization of his boyhood intention to preach the
word of God in the pulpit of some neighborhood church.
As his psychic gifts became known to him, he was driven
at all costs to discover the full meaning of these gifts and
to put them to the best possible use. Once this was accomplished, he could see the shape of his life's work laid out
before him: to make himself and his work at all times
available for investigation by qualified scientists; to make
the accumulating evidence available to all who expressed
interest in the extraordinary truths he was helping reveal; and, finally, after the evidence had been amassed in
irrefutable quantity and quality, to spread the word

among terror-ridden human beings that there was nothing to fear in death.

Except for the heart condition that plagued him the last twenty years of his life, Arthur Ford had the physical constitution of a healthy ox. Though he was not very tall —perhaps five feet nine—his round face, thick neck, heavy shoulders, and thick chest gave him the aspect of a big man. He had great physical strength and, even after he had learned about his heart condition, expended it recklessly.

During the last twenty years of his life he developed a pattern that his friends learned to predict but found themselves powerless to alter. A strenuous round of lecturing would bring him low with a heart attack. There would follow a period of convalescence, after which he would assure everyone that he "never was so fine."

The final two decades of Arthur Ford's life were full of hair-raising close calls. One time, Bill Wilson, the AA co-founder, was walking down the street when he was overtaken by a powerful feeling that "I ought to stop in and see Art Ford." Ford was then living in New York. Bill, who was intent on an important errand, tried to fight off the feeling. But it grew until, Bill told me, "I was practically forced to go over to Arthur's apartment." He found the door open, the phone off the hook, and Ford unconscious on the floor, gasping with a heart attack. Bill, of course, summoned medical help, which fortunately arrived in time.

On another occasion, in Florida, a visitor "just happened to drop in" at a moment when Ford was having another near-fatal heart attack. The visitor "chanced" to be one of the senior members of the Cape Kennedy space medical team and a heart specialist (Ford knew a number of space people and was frequently consulted by one of our moon-walking astronauts).

Another time, a heart attack overtook him in the middle of a séance. The alarmed sitter commanded Fletcher to awaken Ford from his trance—which Fletcher did—and summoned medical help.

These warnings altered Ford's hurry-frenzy-rush-and-collapse pattern not at all. One blustery, near-zero January night, I recall, Arthur gave one of his public lectures to a packed auditorium at Riverside Church, New York. After the lecture, several of us were invited to a friend's apartment a dozen blocks away. Knowing of Arthur's precarious health, a couple of us tried to persuade him to wait in the church until we could find a taxi. Arthur would have none of it and struck out at a brisk pace up the hill in the face of a freezing wind. Halfway there he developed severe pains in his chest. This time, these pains did not develop into a full-fledged heart attack, but he gave us all a scare.

Possessing enormous physical strength, Arthur could never accustom himself to the fact that he was an invalid. One time early in 1968, he came up from Philadelphia, where he was then living, for a conference in my home in Connecticut to plan his book *Unknown but Known*. I met him at the railroad station. I spotted him walking toward me, down the platform, carrying a huge suitcase as easily as a girl might carry her purse. "Here," I said, playing the part of welcoming host, "let me take that." I reached for his suitcase, he let go of it, and it fell to the ground, nearly pulling my arm out of its shoulder socket. "Good God, Art," I said, "what have you got in here? Pig iron?"

"I brought along a few books I thought you might like to see."

"Did your doctor say anything about heavy lifting?" Ford just smiled foolishly and started talking about something else. When the heart attack that came upon him during the first days of 1971 turned out to be his last, none of us who knew him was surprised. He had never learned to take care of himself.

He did, however, have a constant overriding concern about taking care of other people. He had friends in the whole human spectrum from judge to jailbird, and he worried about them all. Except for this brief mention, I will leave his women friends to his biographers. These were sharply divided into two groups, public and personal. Ford was worshiped as saint and guru by hundreds, if not thousands, of women, and he avoided entanglements with them all. In the twenty years I knew him, Arthur had deep commitments to only two women. One of these was terminated by the woman's death of cancer. Arthur was disconsolate and bereft. It was some time before he formed another deep attachment for a woman. This was ended by his own death. Man or woman, once Arthur gave his friendship, it was a lasting and dependable thing.

Some of these friends, unaware of or indifferent to the fact that he was an invalid, made outrageous demands on his time and strength. One time a radio network commentator from New York and I, having heard that Arthur was in trouble, went down to Philadelphia to see what we could do. We found Arthur sick, sampling his own self-prescribed "medicine," and sleepless under the demands of two young men he was "trying to help." One was a schizophrenic, recently out of an upstate New York mental hospital, who had somehow found his way to Ford with a story that awakened Arthur's sympathy —his beautiful young sweetheart had died under the ministrations of a bungling doctor. The other, a brisk young man in his thirties, was an ex-convict, just out from a long penitentiary term for a charge which, he had convinced Ford, was unjust. Neither of them had the sensitivity to see Arthur's need or the competence to do anything about it. They were, the radio man and I thought, sponges of a most inconsiderate sort. But Ford's solicitous friendship went out to them fully as generously as it did to the distinguished Senators, Congressmen, jurists, state governors, and intellectuals who sought him out.

All these might be considered as peripheral to the central interest of the final decade of his life—Spiritual Frontiers Fellowship. Here, he felt, was to be found the best hope for awakening his country from what he regarded as a materialistic trance. With his fellow clergymen of SFF and their following of dedicated scientists, intellectual leaders, gifted psychics, and concerned citizens, he centered his hope and a great part of his activity.

Besides conducting his own mediumship, one of Ford's principal activities was training other promising young psychics to develop their natural gifts and use them with greatest effectiveness. In this, he insisted, the most important thing was concentration. It was his own unusual powers along this line that made it possible for him to

put himself into trance at will. It was through concentration that he also brought to bear his perceptive abilities
such as clairvoyance and precognition. Although he
never thought of himself as a prophet or emphasized
precognition as an important part of his mediumship, a
careful study of his work would reveal almost as many
precognitive "hits" as were rung up by the celebrated
Washington prophetess Jeane Dixon. However, I am
under orders here not to stress his evidential record—
"that has already been done." I am remarking only on his
powers of concentration.

One time, while I was driving him through Connecticut and going on at great length about something, I noticed that he had not responded for some minutes. Looking over at him, I saw that he was deep in his own
reflections. "Sorry, Jerry," he said, "I was trying to find
Pike." This was at the time when Bishop James Pike was
lost in a Middle Eastern desert. Through his clairvoyance, Ford was able to give a description of Pike's situation during the last hours of the bishop's life several
days before Pike's body was found. The strain of such concentration must have been great. I have often speculated
that the intervals of harum-scarum disorganization that
punctuated Arthur's life might have been simply the operation of some kind of psychic safety valve, releasing
him temporarily from the enormous pressure such concentration must have created.

Arthur Ford was a kind of modern St. Andrew—he
found a special joy in introducing people whose meeting
might produce some kind of creative outcome. If a business friend was forming a new company whose possibilities Ford thought were promising, he would do all he

could to find investors for it. If one of his literary friends produced a new book—this happened several times in the course of my friendship with Arthur—he would make sure that people in a position to increase the book's influence and readership got to know about it under favorable auspices. If he thought someone was lonely, or sick, or in any kind of trouble, he would try to arrange introductions that might provide the needed life ingredient. Arthur Ford possessed a very strong sense of what must be called the immediacy of history. History, particularly in its Biblical form, was to him not a dead record of past events, but a lively and perceptive account of the kinds of things that actually go on in our universe, but that modern man, on a materialistic jag which must be brief if he is to survive, has chosen to expunge from the record or completely ignore.

"The whole New Testament," he would say, "properly understood, is an unusually observant record of psychic phenomena, of a kind which still takes place today, occurring around a group of unusual mediums—one of whom was supremely inspired. Telepathy, clairvoyance, apports, telekinesis, and nonmedicinal healing continue today as they did in the times of Francis of Assisi, Jesus of Nazareth, Joseph, and Moses. As one example, even the most materialistic of physicians cannot overlook Alcoholics Anonymous as the outstanding example of faith healing of our time. Medicine failed utterly to slow the ravages of the third largest killer of our time—alcoholism. Psychiatric science did no better. Only AA, using techniques which are neither medical nor psychiatric but purely spiritual, has consistently produced recoveries—and produced them regularly, year in and year out for a third of a century—until now they run into the hundreds of thousands."

Arthur Ford could not escape the feeling that moderns, bedazzled by the flashy and superficial triumph of technology, greatly underrated the wisdom of the ancients and in doing so risked their very survival. Ford, of course, was not alone in this conviction. Remarkable evidence of one of these phenomena—healing—was recorded in a conference at Wainwright House, Rye, New York, which sponsored many important forums at which Ford made many appearances. During the 1950's a Wainwright House conference on spiritual healing drew attendance from as far east as London and as far west as Los Angeles. It was attended by professors of medicine, surgery, and psychiatry from famous schools of medicine; by medical directors of famous hospitals; by trance mediums, faith healers, and psychics; by clergymen; by practicing physicians; and by laymen. All agreed that the phenomenon variously called spontaneous recovery, spiritual healing, and faith healing was a standard and oft-repeated reality of the medical experience of our time, operative in the most feared diseases, as well as the more trivial ones. Ford wanted moderns to take more seriously the testimony of the ancients, not simply because it was ancient and venerable, but because it was essential to our survival that we comprehend it.

Not everything hallowed by time was equally respected by Ford; some of the ancient and medieval notions he considered abominable. In his lectures, he never tired of berating preachers, both ancient and modern, who tried to strike fear into the hearts of their hearers—

particularly children—with horrendous stories of a hell to come for those who misbehaved. Those who knew Arthur well called this tirade his "to-hell-with-hell lecture." There is, perhaps, a biographical reason for Ford's aversion to this kind of thing. Hellfire sermons have always been and still are an important part of a certain stratum of religion in the American South, and Arthur had unquestionably heard his share of them as a boy. He could regale us with tales of sermons he had heard. "There was one old devil who used to tell the schoolchildren, 'If you don't watch your step, that man's gonna come right down off that cross and pick you way up in the air and throw you right down into the hottest, blackest, meanest corner of hell.' " Ford attacked the falsehood and superstition that have come down to us from antiquity as energetically as he defended the ancient knowledge that his own experience led him to believe was true. In regard to this book, his instructions on the historical passages were extensive and explicit. His own experience was summed up in one of his most popular lectures, the substance of which was: "We survive death. We survive death regardless of whether we have been good or bad. We survive with memory, personality, and capacity for recognition."

Ford believed that modern physical science was tragically misguided and fundamentally unscientific and that the adulation heaped upon it by a misled public was in fact the mass worshiping of a false god.

"Physical science has a great deal of know-how but very little know-what or know-why. In analyzing a note, it loses the symphony; in studying an atom, it misses a universe. As a result, it spurs us to do with greater and greater efficiency things that never should have been done in the first place."

If I were given to second-guessing, I might find something "inevitable" in my literary collaborations with Arthur Ford. Certainly we had a lot in common. We had many mutual friends. Each had lost a beloved sister. We both had been married and divorced and tried again. Both had experienced serious brushes with the booze habit. We both loved to swap stories and thoroughly relished pure nonsensical fun. We both had been fired since boyhood with a fascination with the created universe and an endless curiosity about its deep meaning. Both of us were driven by what might be called a sense of public mission. We both felt that humanity had taken a wrong turn and that it was our job to shout a warning. Though we came to it by very different routes, we arrived at the same conclusion regarding modern physical science. In Arthur's education there was almost no natural science; in mine there was such a superabundance that its essential shallowness was forced to my attention and I was driven to seek broader, deeper dimensions. All in all, we seemed to find working together mutually rewarding. Working with this extraordinary man has been one of the great illuminations of my life.

On December 19, 1970, Arthur, aware of the seriousness of his illness, wrote his last letter to me. This—deleting certain irrelevant personal and business details—is the letter:

Box 1149,
South Miami, Florida
December 19, 1970

DEAR JERRY ELLISON:

Since my return from NYC I have been laid low with another heart attack. That explains my long silence. Have had a male nurse and thus was able to avoid another stay in the hospital. I have the book's contract and will sign and return it this weekend. The publishers no doubt will be in touch with you. The material is set, but you will have to organize the book and write it. I am just not up to it. But I do want to get this book out of my system. I think it important. Out of the many thousands of letters that have come to me in the last few years at least 80 percent ask the question: What happens after death? I want this book to be an honest and logical sort of deduction drawn from the serious work that has been done. I do not plan to give a lot of case histories and all that sort of thing. You will know how to handle it. There have been many compliments on the last book.

I hope you will see me through this in the same wonderful way you did with the last one. I imagine this will be my final contribution to the Cause.

My heart condition is not apt to kill me off soon. It is angina, and if I do not do anything too strenuous, I am all right. But it can be very painful, and there are times when I can barely walk. So easy does it.

I am simply ignoring Christmas this year. But I do send you and yours best wishes for a good New Year.

Love to you all,

ART

Certain features of this letter lead me to think it was as much a statement for the record as a personal communication. For one thing, there is a certain formality about it that was not Arthur's usual style in writing me. This is the only note I ever received from him in which I am addressed by first and last name; his usual salutation was simply "Dear Jerry." There is nothing in the letter that had not already been understood between us. I believe he wrote it partly to make sure that I would complete the work that we had begun and partly to provide me with clear evidence that the book was a long-planned and carefully worked-out collaboration. Much more went into it than the few months of planning and discussion that preceded the actual setting down on paper. There is the whole richness of twenty years of Arthur Ford's developing thoughts on the problem of life after death as assimilated by one who knew him well. There is his own selection of preferred sources and the marginalia from his library. There is his own spoken account of his out-of-body experience and of the three times in his life when, in deep coma, he stood at the very door of death. Finally, and conclusively, there are the reports, brought to us through Arthur and Fletcher and through other channels, spoken by those actually living the life that is the subject matter of this book—the life beyond death. It is in all respects a faithful review of the best that is known on this topic, by Arthur Ford as he instructed that it be told.

JEROME ELLISON

I

Vibrations, Evolution, Personal Growth

FOR A TIME after I first made the unsettling discovery that my body could be used as a telephone line from one realm of being to another, I never guaranteed results at my séances. People in the discarnate sector of the spectrum of being are like earth people in this respect: They are people. If they want to come, they come; if they don't, they don't—and sometimes they didn't.

After Fletcher came on the scene to team up with me, results were much more consistent, but still there were complainers. "I'm willing to go along with this stuff," a medium baiter said one tine, "if you'll positively guarantee to bring me Socrates."

"I'll bring you Socrates," I replied, "if you'll positively guarantee that the person I bring you is Socrates."

In this little contretemps is the kernel of one of the most important considerations I want to get across in this book: the factor of personal growth. Would the Socrates of *now* have the same preoccupations and hold to the same doctrines that characterized him in the Fifth century B.C.? Do *you* have the same interests, beliefs, and background of experience you had one, two, three, or four decades ago? This factor of psyche development is one of the keys to gaining a fuller comprehension of those realms of being beyond the earth-biology plane.

The growth impulse that is a human being is an immaterial one. It takes and discards the materials needed for its progressive stages of growth. After a certain stage, human beings on earth stop growing physically. From then on their growth is in the dimension of experience, thought, sensitivity, and awareness—that is, in the *immaterial* dimensions.

Growth in these dimensions requires food of a different kind from that called for in physical growth, and it produces a different kind of strength. Just as a fetus reaches a point where it is strong enough to maintain itself outside its mother's body, so the nonmaterial growth impulse of a "mature" human being reaches a point where it can sustain itself in the more rarefied realm of thought energy—"spirit"—without further dependence on its temporary home, its earth body. Then, exactly as the fetus grew after physical birth and infancy, through childhood and adolescence to full participation in the earth society, so the fledgling spirit makes its way into the company of other spirits in the dimensions and structures of high-energy disembodied thought.

If what I have just said is true—as the weight of evidence clearly indicates—why is it so hard for today's average American mind to accept? The tragic answer—that we have been brainwashed by the false assumptions of our own materialistic technology—has been given elegant utterance by the distinguished philosopher Michael Polanyi, whom I will presently quote at length. For the moment I will make my point in terms of the ordinary rough-and-tumble of American life. The scene, let us say, is the main downtown office of the Continental Boiler Works; the time, Monday morning. H. M. Stern, senior vice-president, is being greeted by Timothy Freejoy, who is arriving at the office five minutes late and in a gay mood.

"Morning, H. M.," says Tim, cheerfully. "How's things with your immortal soul this morning?"

"Mmmfffbblllnnttnn," mumbles Stern.

"Sorry to be late, boss," says Tim, rushing to his desk to begin dutifully shuffling papers, "but my meditation ran a little overtime this morning. You know how it is when you get in real deep. Those higher vibrations really send you, and you can't always break it off right on time."

Stern, obviously, has put Freejoy down as a freak. Mentally, he strikes Timothy from the list of possible promotions next round; promotions can go only to people who can be certified as being of sound mind.

My hypothetical case is lighthearted but not nonsensical. Discussion of immaterial values and phenomena is rigidly censored in materialistic Twentieth-century America. Understanding of these realms dies out from sheer lack of communication; you simply don't talk about such things. This news blackout, of course, affects not at all the created structure of the universe or the facts of human development. What we are doing here—now—is breaking the censorship to convey the basic facts of our lives.

Just to establish them solidly enough to make them readily available for future reference, let us review the main facts of human physical and mental development as given to us by modern scientists. It has been postulated that each of us, in a biological process called recapitulation, actually relives, during the months of fetal growth, the entire experience of organic evolution on earth—fish, reptile, mammal to man. Scientists have also suggested that the entire *psychic* experience of our species is relived during infancy, childhood, and adolescence—the being an animal on all fours; the *pretending* to be an animal; the naïve, superstitious direct acceptance of felt phenomena in the manner of the primitive savage; the hunter phase (actually hunting and killing of small creatures or playing at hunting—reliving the million years when man survived by his prowess as a hunter) ; the warrior phase; and, finally, one hopes, the matured human as an individual of reflective thought and purposive, socially minded action.

The ground we have just been over applies to the individual. The next most important question in understanding the life beyond what we call death concerns itself with the entire species: "How did we come *to be* such creatures?"—beings born into a material world of flesh and growing into a world of pure thought energy or spirit? The scientists have a one-word answer: evolution.

Because evolution is not widely understood, we will take a paragraph or two to review it. Many educated people, still clinging to the nineteenth-century Darwinian concept of physical evolution by natural selection and mutation, have concluded that, since drastic *physical* changes in man have not been observed for a long time, evolution has ceased. The fact is that the evolutionary spearhead has left the realm of the purely physical and entered the area of the psychosocial, where evolutionary changes are going forward at an accelerating rate.

This is the great *scientific* news of our time. The great accomplishment of our century is not the release of atomic energy, which is simply an extension of a search for greater mechanistic power that began three centuries ago. Nor is it putting men on the moon, which is a delayed utilization of mechanical possibilities known to Leonardo da Vinci. The great science news of our century is that man has been given full partnership—and full participating responsibility—in his own evolution.

If it's as important as all that, why hasn't more been heard of it? It's simply a case of poor publicity. Our era pays little attention to discoveries that produce no commercial, medical, or military profit. The pioneers were all lone workers; R. M. Bucke, physician; Samuel Butler, novelist; Henri Bergson, philosopher; C. G. Jung, psychiatrist; Pierre Teilhard de Chardin, paleontologist; Julian Huxley, biologist; H. T. Wieman, theologian. Working alone, some of these men were surprised when they learned that others had made the same discovery: that man participates in his own evolution, and to a rapidly increasing extent. The definitive statement concerning evolution of consciousness was given us by Julian Huxley, the famous British biologist, during the 1940's: "Man is nothing else than evolution become conscious of itself." He explains:

During evolution, awareness (or if you prefer, the mental properties of living matter) become increasingly important to organisms, until in mankind it becomes the most important characteristic of life. . . .

Evolution takes on a new character: it becomes primarily a psychosocial process . . . working through a combined operation of knowing, feeling and willing.

What matters most of all? Those things which increase the human being's capacity for awareness. This business of *being aware* is central to understanding our present life, as well as our lives after our earthside biological functioning has ceased. So let's linger for a page or two over the matter of what is meant by being aware.

First, let's consider the enormous range of sensibility— awareness—among the people we know. In sensitivity to sound, we may place at one extreme the chaps who work in Mr. Stern's hypothetical boiler factory. For most of them, the hearing sense has been so abused by the bang and clatter of boilermaking as almost to obliterate any more delicate appreciation of sound. At the other extreme we may place the symphony-goer, whose trained ear detects the finest shadings of tone in the subtlest musical instruments, as well as tone qualities in nature— bird songs, wind sounds, sea sounds, human speech and song. In a very real sense, there is a world of sound the boilermaker knows nothing about from his own experience and whose worth, possibly whose very existence, he may therefore question.

Who has not suffered at the hands of those who have no sensitivity to human feelings? There is a world of tender human emotion such people know nothing of. Most Americans have no real knowledge of the world of national and international politics, though political events massively affect their lives. Think of the multiple world around us whose existence is unquestioned but concerning which we have little or no knowledge: science, art, music, sports, education, commerce, agriculture, industry, to name only a few. We see at once that our blind spots—our failures to be aware of what actually exists—are not restricted to matters concerning the life beyond death. We find them abundantly in affairs which grossly affect our humdrum, practical earth-side existence. For this reason, those of us who have increased our awareness of the psychic world (or, as in my own case, had such increased awareness thrust upon them!) do not dally long over people's protests that they "hadn't heard about such things." Our job is to do what we can to make sure that they *do* hear about such things. In this we are being strictly scientific, following the leading of Huxley, Jung, and the others. "The purpose of human life," wrote Dr. Jung, "is to increase conscious awareness."

Now, since my purpose is to make my reader *aware* of modes of existence other than the earthbound and fleshly, let us go on with this discussion of awareness. A great deal of our universe—possibly all of it—is made up of energy vibrating in orderly arrangement. We comprehend our world through what we call our five senses, which are the results of vibrations acting on specialized nerve ends which respond to the wave rhythms producing sensations of sight, sound, smell, taste, and touch.

Obviously we have means of detecting many other vibrations and other forces than these five—or, to say the same thing another way, we have many more than five senses. But because science has not got around to naming and classifying these other perceptions, we arbitrarily rule any information that comes to us through them as "extrasensory."

This, of course, is a serious misnomer—serious because its bland acceptance inhibits science from its obligation to identify these other senses and inhibits the rest of us from making full use of them. For example, we have a gravitational-field sense (this is so highly developed in such simple creatures as clams and potato buds that they know at all times—even in the dark and even when buried—where the sun and the moon are). We have a sense of location (so highly developed in birds that they can navigate accurately over thousands of miles without landmarks). And we have a sensitivity to thought (telepathy has been demonstrated so positively that it can no longer be called *extra*sensory; it must be accepted as a fully qualified sixth sense).

When we consider the vast multitude of significant vibrations which surround us at all times and of which we are totally unaware, we see how ridiculous it is to imagine that our "five senses" give us anything like an accurate picture of the universe we live in. Yet our materialistic scientists would have us think that these and only these are the sole source of data from which to derive comprehension!

This matter of vibrations is important to me; I am convinced that becoming aware of the next stage of existence beyond the earth biosphere is very largely a matter of becoming attuned to its vibrations. For the sake of the journey we are about to undertake, I want my readers to become so thoroughly accustomed to the fact that they are surrounded by unrecognized but nonetheless significant vibrations that accommodation to the possibility of one more set—those emanating from other spheres of being—will not be too difficult. A well-trained human ear, for example, can detect sounds within the range of 20 to 20,000 vibrations per second. Every stray dog knows from direct experience that the air is full of exciting sounds on both sides of these limits. Electromagnetic waves? If they are longer than 4/10,000 of a millimeter (violet) and shorter than 7/10,000 of a millimeter (red) we can see them. Of the myriad electromagnetic/waves outside this range—X rays, radio waves, energies of cosmic origin—we are completely unaware. Are they, therefore, of no significance in our lives? Cosmic rays, we are told, have been one of the important causes of the mutations which have been one of the two essential features of classical evolution theory. The contemporary world has become so dependent on electronic communication—radio waves—that it could not function in its present fashion without them. The quasars ("radio stars") have been sending out radio waves since the creation of the stellar universe, but no one knew of such waves until Heinrich Rudolf Hertz discovered them in 1886.

Is it so difficult, then, to conceive of vibrations and wave formations of very great importance to us all which still remain undiscovered by formal science? To those who have made an effort, even a small one, to develop the full range of their perception, there is no question whatever about the reality of these unclassified emanations. I am thinking now of a student of mine who discovered that he could see people's auras—those subtle radiations which many psychics believe emanate from the astral body which will be the individual's home in the next stage of his existence. These emanations are sometimes so powerful that they affect photographic film. Certain people, film manufacturers have found, cannot be permitted to work where fresh film is being produced—their presence exposes the film. Soviet investigators have succeeded in photographing portions of the aura. Aura reading is one of the recognized types of psychic ability. "Why, it's exactly like tuning a radio or TV set," a friend told me excitedly in describing his first experience in perceiving the aura. "When my vision was tuned in on the aura, the regular everyday features of the person seemed blurred. When I tuned my vision to sharp everyday seeing, I could hardly see the aura at all!" This brings us to the most mysterious, most exciting world of all—the world of thought. Is this world, too, made up of vibrations, perhaps too fine, too fast, too penetrating for our instruments to detect?

One thing we do know for certain: Thought can be transmitted from one human mind to another in somewhat the same way that radio waves travel from one station to another. Two generations of controlled human experiments, backed by the extraordinary demonstrations of Cleve Backster with plants, have proved that thought energy easily passes through barriers (thick shieldings of lead, concrete, etc.) that stop all other known forms of energy emission.

But the most exciting thing about thought is its awe-inspiring power to create and destroy. No house was ever built without first coming into existence as an edifice of thought. No bomb was ever dropped except after careful scheming in the chemist's laboratory and at the armorer's drafting board. No doctor, poet, scientist, or opera singer was ever made by nature; they are made only by girls and boys who first think these roles, then, over long years, finally give themselves the shape of their

thoughts. The power of imagination is the power of creation—for good or for ill. If our environment is polluted,
it is simply the result of our polluted imaginations; we
might as easily have imagined and thus created an environment of friendliness and beauty. My point is, of
course, that the intangible world of thought governs and
controls the tangible world of substance. We now find
ourselves in an evolutionary pact with the creative forces
of the universe. What we are and what we will become
will be the result of a joint human and divine imaginative effort. In this effort, the higher realms of being that
lie outside earth's biosphere will have an important part
to play.

Michael Polanyi is a name seldom heard by the man in
the street, but he is well known to every scientist competent enough in his field to be working at the very frontier
of scientific understanding. One of the world's top-
ranking philosophers of science, the eighty-year-old Polanyi has been responsible for breakthroughs in reasoning that could very well reverse the whole trend of
scientific thinking. Mechanistic science, Polanyi says,
made the mistake, more than a century ago, of what my
"cracker" forebears would call grabbing hold of the
wrong end of the animal. Traditional scientists, reasoning that nature works from the simple toward the
more complex, have analyzed simple and natural forms
right down to the very nucleus of the atom in the hope of
discovering nature's secrets. They have found only frus-
tration.

This, according to Polanyi's reasoning, was to be expected. The simple, he argues, can never produce the
more complex. No roomful of pupils can spontaneously

produce a teacher. A ladle of molten iron and a tub of rubber cannot produce an automobile. One cannot comprehend a great poem by concentrating on one of its words. The higher forms of existence, he insists, do not and can never emerge from the lower. What actually happens is the exact reverse: The higher forms of existence exert their influence downward, guiding, governing, and shaping the lower forms. As the Hindus have a way of saying, when you want guidance, you look to your guru, not to your dog. The great secrets of the universe will never be found in the atom, the molecule, or the cell.

"Circumstances operating under lower principles are fixed by higher agencies not under the control of those principles." And again: "the more intangible the matter in the range of these hierarchies, the more meaningful it is." And again: "I criticize all reductionist, mechanistic programs founded on the idea which identifies ultimate knowledge with the lowest level of the universe." And again: "The principle of intelligence is not the ultimate principle or the highest level governing the functioning of living beings. It leaves its powers open to the still higher principle of responsible choice." And again: "There is a multiple hierarchy which leads on to ever more meaningful levels. Each higher level is more intangible than the one below it and enriched in subtlety. As these more intangible levels are understood a steadily deeper understanding of life and man is gained." And again: "The unbridled detailing of mechanistic science destroys our knowledge of the things we most want to know. It gives us a world composed of bits of matter in motion in which nobody lives." And again: "Our theory must endorse the ways we transcend our embodiment by acts of indwelling and extension into more subtle and intangible realms of being."

You can see, now, that what I have been trying to do in this chapter is establish a rationale for a better comprehension of the intangible but real world—and doing it entirely within the idiom of contemporary science. Not that I think for one minute that contemporary science is right. Its positivistic materialism has rendered it all but useless in ministering to the real needs of man. Too large a segment of our scientific establishment has fallen into the hands of small-capacity men who have gained some prestige by mastering a set spiel in a limited area and who have no real knowledge or insight. The true pioneers in scientific thought are not, of course, made in this stripe. I believe that the true philosophers among scientists will follow Polanyi's lead, turn their attention once again to those intangible realms of pure thought energy that shape our universe, and thus restore science once again to its proper role in the leadership and guidance of man.

Why, it may well be asked, if I have such misgivings about the science of our day, have I cast my opening chapter in the language and idiom of that very science? All my data on vibrations, on wave phenomena, on evolution, on personal growth, on cultural progress have been scientific data. The illustrations I have used have been scientific ones; the authorities I have quoted have been scientists. The only philosopher I have quoted is a leading philosopher of science.

I have a reason for this. Every age must speak in the language characteristic of its own time. Our age is the age of materialistic science. I am personally convinced that in the historic long haul, many of our solemnly accepted hypotheses will appear as ridiculous as the debates of the medieval schoolmen on how many angels could establish residence on the head of a pin.

Nevertheless, this is the language of twentieth-century America. We have been reared in it. Our language, our thoughts are steeped in it. If we want to communicate with one another effectively, we must use the language we best understand. I very much want to communicate with you on the subject of the life beyond death. And so I have carefully avoided the specialized vocabulary that has developed to deal with those less tangible realms beyond.

We must realize, however, that ours is not the only vocabulary capable of dealing with significant reality. If we take the word of science that the universe is about 5 billion years old and that man arrived less than 2,000,000 years ago, we see that he appeared late in the evolutionary process. We are newcomers here. From the beginning, man has been involved with the cosmic creative principle—the divine—in a great adventure in the evolution of consciousness. He has never ceased striving to increase his awareness of the totality in which he is involved. The basic realities of this involvement—the growth from cellular to fetal life, through infancy, childhood, adolescence, to socially responsible adulthood, the intimations of states of being beyond earth life, the rare but unforgettable direct insights into that ultimate life—have not changed.

Our modern insights into the ultimate life have, I think, left behind a few superstitions and penetrated a little further into ultimate creative reality. But we are in no position to be patronizing toward ancient beliefs. The ancient thinkers, prophets, and seers were neither naïve nor stupid. We have reason to think that the best of them may have gained ground we may be a long time recapturing. It is well worth our while to review their thinking and feeling and experiencing carefully, sympathetically, and respectfully.

They will not be using our language. Where we speak of statistics, formulas, and data, they are more likely to speak of myths, legends, and parables. Where we think of graphs, research, and computations, we may find them immersed in riddles, folktales, and symbolism. We cannot for these reasons underrate them. They were at least as intelligent as we are. They were up against the same universal realities that we confront. We are not doing so superbly well that we can afford to miss any tricks.

II

The Idea of Survival in Man

WE WHO HAVE been born into the materialistic cultural climate of twentieth-century America carry with us a heavier burden of materialist thinking than perhaps we know. Some may live their entire lives without having this materialism seriously challenged. Others are forced by sheer pressure of events to acknowledge and deal with energies which have no materialistic explanation. My unasked and totally unexpected aptitude as a psychic put me from the beginning in this latter category. The conventional wisdom of my time had no explanation for what was actually happening in my life. It was sometimes extremely confusing, and at such times I was hard put to find competent understanding and guidance.

When in my early twenties I was already in demand to do open clairvoyance as a speaker before spiritualist groups. I had not yet learned to handle trance, but learned that there was a certain wide-awake half-hypnotized state in which I could describe unseen presences and pick up some of their messages for an audience. I was aware of my need for training but meanwhile had to settle for picking up whatever I could learn by practicing on my listeners. The National Spiritualist Association of America, dedicated to "the science, philosophy and religion of continuous life, based upon the demonstrated fact of communication, by means of mediumship, with those who live in the spirit world," provided me with plenty of these. Young, full of zeal, and flush with my first success in a parish of a denomination which could take its religion in a practical straightforward way, it seemed odd to me that people should have to found a special organization to speak candidly about immortality.

Help of a most unusual kind came to me at the time I most needed it. In 1920 the great Hindu sage Paramahansa Yogananda came to Boston to address a convocation of Unitarians. I had heard of him, of course, and luckily, he had heard of me, so I had no trouble arranging a conference with him. I told him of my difficulties in attaining concentration, meditation, and detachment. He understood them immediately and accepted me as a friend and fellow seeker. From then on, I consulted with him whenever I could arrange my schedule to do so.

Yogananda helped me put my psychic abilities in their proper perspective. He respected them but was not overly impressed. Nor would he allow me to make their development my central aim. Mediumistic abilities develop as a matter of course among souls growing toward universal consciousness, he said, warning his students not to be distracted or diverted from their course by them. To Yogananda there was no question about the life beyond death or about the value of modern science within its limited field.

He did, however, chide the scientists for losing the greater wisdom while concentrating on the lesser. "Science remains in a perpetual flux," he said, "valuable in discovering the local laws of the existing illusions of nature, but powerless either to reach finality or to reach the Source." I took to heart Yogananda's reminder that all spiritually advanced souls have some mediumistic powers but that *not* all mediums are spiritually advanced. He advised me never to relax my effort to learn all I could about the actual tangible and intangible structure of the cosmos, whether the sources of the necessary information be ancient or modern.

My own direct experience, combined with the findings of those contemporaries of mine who had done the most careful research into human consciousness beyond death, brought me back to the ancient writers with a new respect. They were not simply imaginative storytellers of a long-gone day. The best of them were careful reporters of observed and experienced phenomena. I reread everything I had ever read before along this line and branched out into areas of ancient literature I had never explored before.

What I was seeking, of course, was corroboration of my own experience and observation in the total history of my kind. If these things I was seeing and experiencing were some new and recent development, that would be one thing. If they were things that had happened or were merely said to have happened, ages ago, and never happened anymore, that would be another. However, if the psychic phenomena with which I was becoming daily more familiar had been going on continuously since the very earliest records of man's life on earth, I was indeed

on to something that had to do with the very structure
and purpose of the universe itself and that contained the
key to understanding the essential nature and ultimate
purpose of the human experience. What, I wanted to
know, was the actual history of the idea of survival in
man?

It seemed to me that if the reports of a life beyond
death were to be taken seriously, four essential points
would have to be established. First, there would have to
be a demonstration of a continuing consciousness, with
consciousness defined as perception, memory, recognition, reason, a capacity for decision, and that whole
complex of character overtones we lump together in the
word "personality." Second, some kind of setting would
have to be presented, at least roughly comparable to our
earth on the flesh-biological plane, as a social and natural
environment in which personality might operate. Third,
some kind of life value, goal, necessity, purpose or service
stated in terms comprehensible at our present level of
being would be required. Finally, there would have to be
some kind of answer to the social and ethical situations—
matters of constructive and destructive personalities, justice and injustice, intelligent and slow, vicious and cooperative, brash or timid—that we find so hard to manage
in our present life. What has man had to say, in terms of
his writings on the afterlife, about these things?

The Neanderthals and the Cro-Magnon men of 75,000
to 25,000 years ago believed that the dead live on in some
kind of mysterious spirit body. They were buried with a
tender consideration of what they might need in their
future lives—particularly food and tools. As time went
on, the belief grew stronger that the dead survive in some

real sense; funeral preparations and provisions for burial grew more and more elaborate. By 10,000 B.C. tomb building had begun. Kings, chieftains, and other important people were well provided with things that might be useful in the afterlife. In some cases there was the cruel custom of sacrificing wives and servants, so that the important man might have company and solace on his spirit journey.

It was acknowledged not only that the dead have a way of sometimes turning up on earth again, but also that their personalities while on the earth plane covered the whole range from kindly and cooperative to hateful and destructive. In order to keep the dead from "walking," the corpse may have had a stake driven through it to pin it to the earth, or it may have been tied with strong ropes or covered with heavy stones. At the same time, various offerings were made to assure the dead that they were still held in affectionate memory and otherwise contribute to their contentment. People who had been bad-tempered and malicious in earth life were thought of as demons; generous, brave, and noble people came to be numbered among the benevolent gods. Some primitive groups had quite definite ideas about the movement of the soul during the interval just following death. One tribe believed that the soul moved very much in the way described in James Agee's mid-twentieth-century novel *A Death in the Family*: lingering for a while at the grave; passing briefly among familiar persons and places; then going on to a farther destination.

In Homer's *Odyssey*, I found the first full account of a séance that corresponds with contemporary psychic experience and fulfills all four of the requirements I have set as the minimum necessary to establish personal survival of death. Its appearance in Homer's work gives it a special weight, since this poet was known for his faithfulness in reporting the actual customs, rituals, beliefs, clothing, weapons, structures, and scenes of his time. Reading it, one can hardly question that this ancient poet had attended many séances and based his imaginative account on actual experience.

In *The Odyssey*, the séance scene appears in Book Eleven, which is subtitled "The Book of the Dead." Circe —a kind of prophetess well known and widely publicized in our own time—has advised the hero Odysseus to muster his mediumistic talents and techniques to get in touch with the dead Theban poet Tiresias for advice on his next move. Circe, herself a powerful medium, gives Odysseus exact directions concerning the invocation of spirits. (This is the first historical instance I know of in which one medium has trained another, as I have helped in the training of so many young twentieth-century mediums. But we don't use sheep's blood anymore!) Tiresias, says Circe, has "understanding even death has not impaired" and will be an incalculable help.

Odysseus follows directions carefully. These embody the primitive belief that souls of the dead can somehow utilize some ingredient, tangible or intangible, of foodstuffs—so Odysseus, while calling the dead from Hades, sprinkles the ground liberally with barley, honey, and sheep's blood. The nearest modern parallel I have been able to find is the opinion of some twentieth-century parapyschologists that the ectoplasm and odic force which make apparitions and other physical manifestations possible is an intangible element of the bloodstream, temporarily drawn upon while these phenomena are occurring. Since my experience with psychic phenomena of the physical category has been limited, I cannot comment on this from my own experience. However, the mental aspects of Homer's séance correspond with those of contemporary experience.

Hades, in the Homeric meaning of the word, has none of the connotations of lasting misery which accompany the medieval notion of hell. Hades is simply the spiritual environment where the souls of the dead live. It is to be found on the far side of a "river of fear"—Homer's poetic image for the fear of death which is so common among human beings of all epochs.

The spirits lose no time in appearing after Odysseus has called them. I found it interesting that the first spirit Odysseus encounters is an exact counterpart of a transaction which is very common in contemporary psychic practice—an accurate account of the exact manner of an accidental death, the details of which have been unknown to earth-side survivors. The first spirit to appear is Odysseus' shipmate Elpenor, whom Odysseus had last seen, alive and well, back at Circe's palace. Odysseus wants to know what happened. "It was all the wine I had swilled before I went to sleep," Elpenor explained. "When I awoke I clean forgot to go down to the long ladder and take the right way down, and so fell headlong from the roof. My neck was broken and my soul came down to Hades." It would be easy to find a thousand Elpenors in the records of twentieth-century psychic phenomena.

Ulysses sees a great number of souls—"fresh brides, unmarried youths, old men with life's long suffering be-

hind them, tender young girls still nursing this first an-
guish in their hearts, and a great throng of warriors
killed in battle, their wounds gaping and their armor
stained with blood"—but speaks with only a few: Elpenor, his mother, and the target of his séance, Tiresias. Tiresias gives him the required directions, and the séance
ends.

The Greeks of pre-Hellenic times thought the dead
lived on in an underground world which was in charge of
a Great Goddess or Earth Mother. There was an island
paradise to which the souls of the dead had to be transported by ferryboat. During the Hellenic period, it was
believed that the soul (psyche) was transformed into the
eidolon, a tenuous insubstantial image of the earth appearance of the person. This, in Homer's *Odyssey*, is what
so perturbs Odysseus on meeting, during the séance, his
dead mother Anticlea. The Greek warrior, after trying
vainly to hold her shadowy form in his arms, exclaims,
"Is this but a phantom [eidolon] that Queen Persephone has sent me, that I may lament and groan the
more?" His mother reassures him: "Persephone, daughter of Zeus, does not deceive thee, but this is the way with
mortals when they die."

In very early primitive religions, the one god, creator
of all things and source of all being, though acknowledged and revered, had little to do with the actual lives
of human beings, in either this world or the next. Primitive peoples were much more concerned with the immediate business of obliging the benevolent souls of the
departed and protecting themselves against the malicious
ones. This began to change with the Egyptians, who
came to see life, in this world and beyond, for both king

and commoner, as a steady development in under-standing, a generally happy experience. They intuited a progressive development of the spirit which might eventually lead to personal relationship with the creator himself. During the pyramid-building days, it was thought that the statuettes and miniatures buried with the corpse in the tomb would later be utilized, in their own essences or souls, to do the bidding of the dead man.

The oldest full-fledged concept of the life beyond death was Egyptian. The Egyptian *Book of the Dead* contains full directions concerning what must be done to make the best happen in the afterlife. The kingdom of Osiris envisions a happy and purposeful after-earth existence. The soul sets out, staff in hand, on its long trip toward the Osirian fields, which were considered to be in the general direction of the Milky Way, the Great White Nile of the sky. According to the *Book of the Dead*, not everyone deserves immediate and eternal bliss; at the penultimate stage of the journey, the soul is brought into the Hall of Truth, there to be judged by Osiris. The soul, in his own defense, may present a list of the sins and crimes it did not commit. But the judgment is impartial, and once it is made, the soul must proceed either to the joys of the Osirian fields or to those places where stern correctional treatment is meted out. At one point, the Egyptians briefly achieved the exalted religious concept of the one true god, with whom each human being might aspire to ultimate friendship, through progressive stages of growth in the afterlife.

From the Egyptian *Pyramid Texts* comes a great deal of information about the Egyptian ideas of the afterlife as far back as 4000 B.C. These writings, intended to ensure the safe passage of the dead Pharaohs to the next world, infer two entities, the ka and the ba, which survive the physical body. The ka seemed to have some kind of tenuous physical substance, but the ba was pure spirit or soul. It was always represented in art as a human-headed bird —the person himself, but now capable of free and unobstructed flight. In illustrations for the Egyptian *Book of the Dead,* which dates from around 1450 B.C., the ba is frequently shown perched over the door of the tomb or flying down the tomb shaft to visit the embalmed body below. In its concept of the human being as a psychophysical organism, the ancient Egyptians view of human nature and destiny is surprisingly modern. That the human being was at all times much more than flesh and blood was taken as an established fact.

The very ancient kingdoms of Sumer and Akkad, like the Egyptians, regarded man as a psychophysical being. In this Mesopotamian culture the word *napistu* (throat) was also used to denote breath, life, soul—the animating principle of life, or holy spirit. The individual postmortem personality, called the *etimmu,* if abused or neglected might return, it was thought, to bedevil the living. This belief is the basis of the importance, found in all ancient cultures (for example in Sophocles' play *Antigone*), attached to suitable burial rites. People whose physical bodies had not been disposed of with due ceremony were thought to have been condemned by afterworld authorities to continual wandering until these amenities had been taken care of. Here, readers of the classics will recall the faithful promises of both Odysseus and Aeneas to find and bury, with proper formality, the bodies of departed friends with whom they had spoken in séance. The ancient Mesopatamian afterworld was known as the Land of No Return.

In India, the ancient Vedic beliefs of 4,000 and 5,000 years ago did not include the concept of karma and reincarnation which were later to be so prominent in this region. Man lived in the here and now, which were to be enjoyed to capacity, both physically and emotionally, and continued in his existence in a postmortem phase whose quality was dependent on his moral conduct.

Besides the great organized religions of antiquity, there were innumerable mystery cults scattered through the known world from the dark forests of Germany, through the sunny peninsulas of the Mediterranean and the plains of Asia Minor to the borders of India. These included the Druids of the British Isles, the cult of Waden in what is now Germany, the Eleusinian and Dionysian mysteries of the Greek peninsula, and the dire human-sacrifice cults in Asia Minor which were such "abominations" to the high-minded cult of Yahweh among the Middle Eastern Hebrew tribes. In Greece these cults were called mysteries because their rites were secret—known only to initiates. Candidates for participation underwent long preparation, careful instruction, and solemn initiation ceremonies. The Pythagorean brotherhood, which made notable contributions to our understanding of medicine, music, astronomy, mathematics, and philosophy, had its origin in the Eleusinian mysteries. The Pythagorean studies, designed to encourage such divinity of thought in the earth body that a high state of spiritual purity and insight might be enjoyed in the afterlife, had a lasting effect on religious thought which has persisted throughout the Christian Era and continues to the present day.

Not all these cult religions, of course, were so exalted. The average Greek of this period was given to understand that the afterlife was a well-organized affair, in which, after being judged, the soul passed through a corridor called Erebus, thence, if he were found unworthy, to the unhappy lower regions called Tartarus, or, if he were judged deserving, to a place of joy and blessedness called the Elysian Fields.

Some of these cults carried such a powerful assurance of a successful and altogether livable life after death that Plutarch, more than half a century after the Christian Era had arrived, could write to his wife, upon receiving news of the death of one of his daughters, these comforting words: "About that which you have heard, dear heart, that the soul once departed from the body vanishes and feels nothing, I know that you give no belief to such assertions because of those sacred and faithful promises given in the mysteries of our religious brotherhood. We hold it firmly for an undoubted truth that our soul is incorruptible and immortal. We are to think of the dead that they passed into a better place and a happier condition. Let us behave ourselves accordingly, outwardly ordering our lives, while within, all should be purer, wiser, incorruptible."

Until approximately the fifth century B.C., ideas about the afterlife grew out of widely shared national and tribal experiences which had in the course of time been cast into set forms. Later insights tended to be centered on the teachings of great spiritual leaders who gave new, living meanings to old teachings and ignited in the hearts of their hearers the fires of unquenchable spiritual enthusiasms. Among these were the Persian Zoroaster (sixth century B.C.), Buddha and Confucius (both of the fifth century B.C.), the Hebrew prophets (fifth through the first century), Jesus of Nazareth, and Mohammed (seventh century A.D.). The origins of the lofty and diverse religions of India are lost in the mists of prehistory. The historic record begins to take shape in the great religious verses of the eighth through the sixth century B.C.—the Vedas and Upanishads. These speculations on the origin of all things from one god and the destination of all things in the one god are among the most exalted and penetrating of all religious writings. Here was first pronounced the thought that the *true* self of each individual and the great universal Self are found to be one whenever this unity can be brought into full realization.

The man who was called the Buddha—"The Enlightened One"—bore the given name Siddhartha and the family name Gautama, and was born in northern India about 560 B.C. He enjoyed the religious training and education given the son of a wealthy family of this place and time, grew to manhood, married, had a child—and then, finding no answer to the deep questions of his life in this regimen, took to the road as a solitary and penniless monk to discover, if he could, the meaning of human life. When he had become a matured religious sage, his teachings overthrew the dead regime of an uninspired and decadent religious bureaucracy, reaffirmed the ancient insights of a living religion, and brought new inspiration to the religious life of the Orient.

Buddha sought some way to break the endless chain of painful death and rebirth—the wheel of karma—that led endlessly from one reincarnation to another. He did not question the life after death. But what sense did it make, he asked, if all were simply to be done over again? At last he gave his answer: universal love. This alone could break the wheel of karma and bring one to union with the divine and eternal. Some of his teachings anticipated Jesus' Sermon on the Mount five centuries later: "If someone curses you, you must repress all resentment, and make the firm determination, 'My mind shall not be disturbed, no angry words shall escape my lips, I shall remain kind and friendly, with loving thoughts and no secret spite.'"

The priests felt they had a clear vision of life after death. The Buddhist saint, by consistently following the eightfold path of virtue, was expected to conquer the "three intoxications"—ignorance, sensuality, and the "thirst" which leads to rebirth and repetition. He was presumed now to possess the higher insight and spiritual energy which were beyond any pressing curiosity concerning the life beyond. This position of the master left so many questions unanswered that Buddhism eventually split into sects following several different doctrines. The Buddha's teachings rapidly spread from India into Tibet and into China, where the teachings of Confucius had taken a strong hold.

Few were ever expected to arrive at the state of perfection required to be a Buddhist saint, and there was no question under this teaching that the ordinary individual did survive death. The master used an unforgettable image in expressing his idea of the relationship between the physical body and the earth character with the world beyond. "It is like a metal seal leaving its impression on soft wax," he said. "The metal is left behind; the impression goes on."

In China, from very early times, there had come down a belief that the universe was energized by two contrasting and complementary modes of power—the masculine, active, radiant yang and the receptive, fertile, mysterious yin. The means of utilizing and cooperating with these forces, the governor which kept all things in harmony including the inner life of man, was called Tao—"The Way." Ancestor worship and a detailed concept of the manner of life after death that went with it, were very well entrenched in China. The main work of man was conceived in achieving, through Tao, harmony between men and spirits. In ancient China, prayers and sacrifices were demanded by the ancestors, who were regarded as capable of retaliation if displeased. The spirits did not eat the food, of course, but inhaled and derived sustenance from its essence. After the ceremony, the food was consumed by priests. Wealthy and powerful families had elaborate and sometimes cruel funeral services when an important man died; sometimes from 100 to 300 human victims were sacrificed to provide attendants for the great man in the next world.

This kind of thing the sensible Confucius regarded as outrageous. His teaching could be summarized in the idea "Live a good life in this world and the next one will take care of itself." His idea was that a person who was in harmony with the great creative principles of the universe would be equally at home in all spheres, now and hereafter. Once, in a moment of danger, he said,

"Heaven produced the power that is in me; what have I to fear?" Though Confucius never spoke in detail of the nature of the life beyond, he fully endorsed the traditional Chinese practices of keeping in spiritual touch with ancestors.

For our own time, perhaps the most interesting offshoot of Buddhism is *The Tibetan Book of the Dead*. Since the first publication of the English translation, edited by W. Y. Evans-Wentz in 1927, with its thoughful prefaces by C. G. Jung and other authorities, this remarkable volume has sold through several editions and is now widely distributed as a paperback. It is widely read and discussed among those younger Americans of our time who have interested themselves in meditative techniques of apprehending reality.

The Tibetan Book of the Dead is a how-to-do-it book on the subject of dying. It was used in Tibet as a breviary and read aloud on the occasion of death. Unlike the Egyptian *Book of the Dead*, which was placed in the tomb as a guide for the soul's journey, the Tibetan book is intended as a guide not only for the dying and the dead, but also for the living. A few quotes from the prefatory material emphasize the central theme that the achievement of a proper attitude about dying is one of the central purposes of living: "Thou shalt understand that it is a science most profitable, and passing all other sciences, for to learn to die"; "learn to die and thou shalt learn to live. . . . The exploration of man's inward life is incomparably more important than the exploration of space. To stand on the moon adds only knowledge of things transitory. But man's ultimate goal is transcendence over the transitory. . . . Since all mankind must

relinquish fleshly bodies and experience death, it is
supremely profitable that they should know how rightly
to meet death when it comes." . . . "Let us not fritter
away in worthless doings the supreme opportunity
offered by human birth, lest we depart this life spiritually empty-handed." . . . "This concerns the art of
going out from the body, or of transferring the consciousness from the earth plane to the afterdeath plane."
. . . "An earth-limited medical science has no word of
guidance to convey to the dying concerning the after-
death state, but frequently augments rather than amelio-
rates the unfounded fears and extreme unwillingness to
die of its deathbed patients, to whom it is likely to have
administered stupefying drugs and injections." . . .
"The transition from the human plane of consciousness,
in the process called death, can be and should be accom-
panied by solemn joyousness."

Because it is based on a firm belief in repeated incarnations, the first impact of the Buddhist approach to death
is likely to seem strange to the Western mind. However,
if we deliberately set aside this feeling of strangeness and
consider only those parts of Buddhist wisdom which are
not dependent on a strict interpretation of reincarnation,
we find much that can be creatively applied in our own
framework of thinking. Later on in this book we will dis-
cuss the possibility that reincarnation is but one of several possible solutions to one of the central conceptual
problems concerning the afterlife. For now, let us meet
the Tibetan Buddhist on his own terms.

"It may be argued," writes the lama Anagarika Go-
vinda in one of the prefatory pieces, "that nobody can
talk about death with authority who has not died, and

since nobody has ever returned from death, how can anybody know what happens after it?" He answers that all of us have returned from death since we all have experienced many deaths and reincarnations. The fact that only a privileged few can remember previous incarnations is not evidence that they did not happen. Almost nobody can remember his most recent birth, which assuredly did happen!

But the authority for *The Tibetan Book of the Dead* rests not alone on the insights of the gifted few who can remember previous lives. Learned lamas, Tibetan Buddhist priests and monks, spent their lives contemplating this world and the next, and anticipated their own deaths as the culminating experience of their lives. As death approached, they reported their actual experiences of dying to attending pupils and colleagues. Thus, a very considerable literature of moment-of-death experience is reported by highly trained observers who were fully capable of being objective about their own passing. This material, added to insights attained mediumistically and inspirationally, is the basis on which the breviary is based.

According to this book, the critical instant for the soul occurs immediately after death. At the moment of death, the "Primary Clear Light" is seen. At this moment, the recently deceased is in the actual presence of the creative center of all things: "Now thou art experiencing the Radiance of the Clear Light of Pure Reality," the priest, reading from the breviary by the side of the body, tells the newly released soul. "Recognize it. Oh nobly born, thy present awareness, in real nature void, not formed into anything as regards characteristics or color, is the

very Reality, the All-Good." He is then given the astonishing news that this divine radiance, this "intellect
itself, unobstructed, shining, thrilling," is one with his
own consciousness. "The union of them is the state of
perfect enlightenment." At this precious instant, the soul
must summon all its resources to realize this profound
truth. If this realization can be seized and made permanent, the soul need never die and be reborn again. He is
now at one with God and sharing the work of God along
with the other great enlightened ones.

But if, because of lack of preparation, inattention, or
simply because he has not yet progressed to the degree of
spiritual development where union with the divine is
possible, this moment slips away, it will not come again
until the next death following his next incarnation. Souls
who have missed the supreme moment must now proceed
along a downward scale of states of consciousness until
they arrive at a fertilized womb which will permit them
to be reborn at a level of being appropriate to their
karma—that state of consciousness which is the result of
all their actions through all their incarnations.

The states of consciousness of the soul during the period between death and the next rebirth, as described in
The Tibetan Book of the Dead, are in surprising agreement with after-death testimony offered by modern researchers, both Eastern and Western, who do not endorse
the doctrine of reincarnation. For example: "When the
consciousness-principle getteth outside the body, it
sayeth to itself 'am I dead or am I not dead?' It cannot
determine. It seeth its relatives and friends as it had been
used to seeing them before." It can even hear them but
cannot communicate with them. Three or four days after

death the soul faints away through fear. "Then, when thou wert recovered from the swoon, thy Knower must have risen up in its primordial condition and a radiant body, resembling the former body must have sprung forth—as the Tantra says, 'having a body seemingly fleshly resembling the former and that to be produced, endowed with all sense faculties and power of unimpeded motion, possessing miraculous powers, visible to pure celestial eyes of like nature.' This body, 'born of desire' is a thought form in the intermediate state, and it is called the desire-body."

Evidence of the "desire-body" has, of course, been reported from many quarters besides the Buddhists. Evans-Wentz tells of a European planter who died in the jungles of southwest India and was buried there. Years later, a friend visiting in the area found the grave fenced in and covered with empty whiskey and beer bottles. The local people explained that the dead sahib's ghost had caused so much trouble that some way had had to be found to quiet it. The local witch doctor gave the diagnosis: The ghost, such a heavy drinker in the flesh that the habit caused his death, craved alcohol. The local people, though teetotalers on religious principles, bought the former drinker's favorite brands of beer and whiskey and poured them on the grave to keep the ghost quiet. This was expensive, but, said the locals, it worked!

III

Desert Prophet
Through Emanuel Swedenborg

THE PAST forty years of my life experience have left me without the alternative of debating the question whether the individual personality survives death. I have lived day and night, during these years, in the presence of irrefutable evidence for the affirmative. Indeed, I had resolved not even to bring up the matter in this book; as John Haynes Holmes has said, "the evidence for survival is in."

Nevertheless, living in a skeptical, materialistic world brings contacts which call for resolutions. First, a seriously uninformed and grossly misinformed public needs at all times to be dealt with. In addition, my work has attracted the close attention of scientists of every kind and shade of opinion, and so I have had a heavy exposure to their views. Because both public and scientific opinion affects our general intellectual climate, and hence the set of mind with which we approach my present topic—the actual *conditions* of life after leaving the earth plane—I digress for a moment to review some long-standing predilections.

Scientists, I have found, are not always scientific. The denunciations of the evidence offered by parapsychology by men of science have come almost altogether from people who have never examined the evidence with care. Some of them, however, have remained faithful to scientific method and studied the actual phenomena. Among such men are numbered some of the most vigorous and effective proponents of the fact of survival.

"The very word 'medium' at once brings to our minds the innumerable instances of demonstrated fraud perpetrated by charlatans to extract money from the credulous bereaved," said Brown University's distinguished philosopher and professor emeritus Curt J. Ducasse on the occasion of one of the Foerster Lectures at the University of California. Professor Ducasse, a past president of the American Philosophical Association, goes on to say: "But the modes of trickery and sources of error, which immediately suggest themselves to us as easy, natural explanations of the seemingly extraordinary facts, suggest themselves just as quickly to the members of the research committees of the Society for Psychical Research. Usually, these men have had a good deal more experience than the rest of us with the tricks of conjurors and fraudulent mediums, and take against them precautions far more strict and ingenious than would occur to the average skeptic. To accept the hypothesis of fraud or malobservation would often require more credulity than to accept the facts reported.

"Only two hypotheses at all adequate to explain these facts have yet been advanced. One is the hypothesis of telepathy—that is, the supposition, itself startling enough, that the medium is able to gather information directly from the minds of others, and that this is the true source of the information communicated. To account for all the facts, however, this hypothesis has to be stretched very far, for some of them require us to suppose that the medium can tap the minds even of persons far away and quite unknown to him, and can tap even the subconscious part of their minds. The other hypothesis is that the communications really come, as they purport to do, from persons who have died and have survived death. In the fact of the strong empirical evidence of survival, we need to revise rather radically our ordinary ideas of what is and is not possible in nature."

Columbia University's famous professor of psychology Gardner Murphy, now affiliated with the Menninger Clinic and the esteemed president of the American Society for Psychical Research, has published a painstaking study of cases where information was delivered that, in his opinion, allowed no other conclusion than that it was communicated by a person presumed to be dead. A father, appearing in an apparition to one of his sons sometime after the father's "death," told the existence and location of an unsuspected second will which was then found in the place indicated. A girl appeared as an apparition to her brother nine years after her death, with a conspicuous scratch on her cheek. Their mother then revealed to him that she had made the scratch herself while preparing her daughter's body for burial, but that she had then, at once, covered it with powder and never mentioned it to anyone. An apparition appeared to a general of the British army in India of a lieutenant he had not seen for two or three years. The lieutenant was riding a brown pony with black mane and tail. He was much stouter than at their last meeting and now wore a carefully fashioned beard, whereas he had been clean-shaven. On inquiry, he learned that the lieutenant had indeed become very bloated before his death and had grown exactly such a beard as described. He had bought and ridden to death a pony of the kind that appeared in the apparition.

The evidence for survival is, of course, both endless and conclusive. I cite these cases not because they are the most persuasive but because they underscore the differences between scientists who consider the evidence and "scientists" who do not. The main reason for this split in scientific opinion is, I believe, that the lower echelons of present-day men of science are following a philosophy that has been demonstrated to be at least a century out of date. The logical-positivist philosophy of Auguste Comte, who died in 1857, was for a hundred years the favorite of those who would like to think of the universe as a machine operating strictly according to the laws of classical physics and chemistry and making itself knowable exclusively through man's five gross senses. Since the most important scientific discoveries of the intervening century could not have been made without the help of other senses than these five, Comte's philosophy has been found wanting. The way has once again been opened to allow for the higher senses and faculties of man and still remain within the requirements of scientific correctness.

Besides my direct encounters with several modes of scientific thought, there was one other association—that with Paramahansa Yogananda—that jolted me out of the rather narrow rural Christianity of my boyhood. One had only to meet Yogananda to realize at once that he was in the presence of a very great man—a man of profound learning, unassailable integrity, absolute courage, and endless compassion. Yet this tremendous personality had developed entirely outside the Judeo-Christian tradition! His teaching affected me so deeply that I was jolted into a sharper awareness of the fact that deep and true wisdom might arise in other quarters than the local culture into which I had happened to be born—a culture that turned out to be surprisingly narrow in some important respects. These encounters led me to more extensive reading in the history of the thought of other peoples. When I returned to the Judeo-Christian beliefs of my own time and place, I did so with a greatly enriched understanding.

Returning now to our subject, the conditions of existence in the world after death, we find that the Old Testament Hebrews were pioneers not only in affirming and describing this world, but also in the discovery of one God in nature and the social process. During the two centuries immediately before Christ, the Palestinian Jews were exposed to Greek, Zoroastrian, Babylonian, and Persian ideas that somewhat altered their ancient conception of the life after death. Formerly it had been thought that the dead went to Sheol, a state of shadowy and colorless existence corresponding to the Greek Hades. Now a great many Jews were talking of an afterlife with a restored body full of mental vigor and awareness. Whereas formerly there had been little distinction of merit, now there was reference to the state of the blessed as "paradise," the "Garden of Eden," "Abra-

ham's bosom," or "Under the Throne." Hebrew writings
of this time mentioned "Abraham whom God planted in
the garden of paradise," "Our master Moses departed
into the Garden of Eden," "The holy Judah in Abraham's bosom." All these images contain positive, energiz-
ing elements: a continuance of active personality, a lively
awareness, personal interchange and activity, and surroundings full of possibilities for beauty and delight.
The Jews were not now in agreement—nor had they ever
been—on the nature of the afterlife, but these new elements produced a new excitement about its possibilities.

The ancient Hebrews, despite the fulminations of the
prophets against "wizards (astrologers) and mediums,"
were aware of the relationships between incarnate and
discarnate beings and frequently bridged the gap through
mediums. A notable instance, the séance of King Saul
with the female medium at Endor, clearly demonstrates
that the Jews of Saul's time knew that the personality survived death with memory, recognition, intelligence and
the other attributes of active personality. The Bible reports the incident in some detail:

> Then said Saul unto his servants, Seek me a woman
> that hath a familiar spirit, that I may go to her, and
> inquire of her. And his servants said to him, Behold,
> there is a woman that hath a familiar spirit at Endor.
> And Saul disguised himself, and put on other raiment,
> and he went, and two men with him, and they came to
> the woman by night: and he said, I pray thee, divine
> unto me by the familiar spirit, and bring me him up
> whom I shall name unto thee. And the woman said
> unto him, Behold, thou knowest what Saul hath done,
> how he hath cut off those that have familiar spirits,

and the wizards, out of the land: wherefore then lay-
est thou a snare for my life, to cause me to die? And
Saul sware to her by the Lord, saying, as the Lord
liveth, there shall no punishment happen to thee for
this thing. Then said the woman, Whom shall I bring
up unto thee? And he said, Bring me up Samuel. And
when the woman saw Samuel, she cried with a loud
voice; and the woman spake to Saul, saying, Why hast
thou deceived me? for thou art Saul. And the king said
unto her, Be not afraid: for what sawest thou? And
the woman said unto Saul, I see a god ascending out
of the earth. And he said unto her, What form is he
of? And she said, An old man cometh up; and he is
covered with a mantle. And Saul perceived that it was
Samuel, and he stooped with his face to the ground,
and bowed himself.

And Samuel said to Saul, Why hast thou disquieted
me, to bring me up? . . .

The Jewish worshipers of Yahweh have left us, in the
Bible, the history of a religion in evolution, during
which various ideas of the afterworld, or absence of it,
held sway for a time and passed to give way to new ones.
From the second century B.C. onward, many Jews accepted the view of the soul as the essential self, preexist-
ing the body and surviving it. Mixed with this view was a
resurrectionist teaching that the physical body itself, or a
reasonable facsimile of it, would ultimately have to be restored to provide a satisfactory afterlife.

Jesus of Nazarath spoke of the life beyond death in a
way no one else ever had. He spoke of these realms, to
most people so remote, with the definiteness and authority of one who had actually traveled in them. He deliberately avoided describing afterlife scenes in any great de-

tail "because," as he said, "you could not bear it." Apparently he did not feel that the simple, direct minds of the disciples were then ready to cope with the complexity that a thorough understanding of the afterlife would involve. Also, he made it clear that he did not want speculations on the life beyond to interfere with vital work needing to be done in the immediate present. His teachings always stressed the imperative here and now. A life lived in progressive, loving understanding from day to day, he implied, would lead into a satisfactory continuance without excessive brooding on it.

Jesus did, however, often lift the curtain for a glimpse of what was beyond. "In my Father's house are many mansions: if it were not so, I would have told you." Here we have a glimpse of an unlimited range of conditions and states of consciousness attainable in the higher orders of being. He never ceased to emphasize the importance of the present life as an arena for spiritual development. There is, for example, the report of the beggar Lazarus and the rich man Dives. Both men are described in the afterlife not long after their deaths. Dives' brothers are still living in our sphere, and he is aware of their actions. Dives is having a difficult adjustment to his new conditions; he can no longer get his own way simply by making his wishes known; money, in this new dimension of being, no longer buys clear sailing. Lazarus, however, has put his earthly suffering to good use in maturing his character; he finds himself "in Abraham's bosom." It is interesting to note that Jesus gave very little authority for the kind of "hell," as a place of torment and punishment for sin, that was so widely used by Christian priests of medieval times and later to strike terror into the hearts of their parishioners. Dives, presumably, had as much chance as anybody else of making spiritual progress once he rid himself of the false notions that had been holding him back. The new "Hades" is given us as an intermediate resting place—a kind of checkpoint—where journeying spirits pause for an assessment of their needs and guidance toward their further development. Jesus Himself, according to that early Christian consensus known as the Apostle's Creed, "descended" there before appearing after the Crucifixion in His spiritual (often called "astral") body.

By way of enlightening those of his disciples he thought could "bear it," Jesus, a very great medium, included them in a séance at which Moses and Elijah appeared. The witnesses—Peter, James, and John—were lastingly impressed by the radiant quality of life achieved after biological death by spiritually advanced persons.

Again, when Jesus and the penitent thief were nailed to boards and approaching the extreme agony of crucifixion, Jesus could say, with confidence, "today you will be with me in Paradise." Paradise, in the sense the word was used by Jews of this time, was not the same as that close proximity to the Creator designated as heaven. It was one of the names for the immediate reststop after death. This well-attested speech once again affirmed the afterlife in all its phases as a place where people live in full consciousness and recognize one another.

The Apostle Paul had some significant comments bearing on the relationship between the present life and the life beyond death. "I know a man," he wrote, "who was caught up into the third heaven." He knew another man "who was caught up into Paradise." Apparently Paul himself would have liked to have experienced such revelations. He prayed over the matter. Instead, "there was given to me a thorn in the flesh, the messenger of Satan to buffet me, lest I should not be exalted above measure." Therefore, Paul said, he would glory in his weaknesses, so that the power of spirit might be shown to even greater advantage by appearing in such a faulty vessel. Here I am reminded of those workers in Alcoholics Anonymous who, by "glorying" in their susceptibility to addiction, have done such notable work among the sick alcoholics of our time.

Paul made other references to the ability of some persons to perceive dimensions of reality which he could not. "Concerning spiritual gifts," he wrote, "there are diversities." He lists among these gifts the ability to discern spirits (mediumship), wisdom, knowledge, faith, the gift of spiritual healing, prophecy, linguistic ability, and performing miracles. But (and here I am reminded of Yogananda's admonition) none of these gifts in themselves indicate true spiritual advancement; without loving understanding, Paul says, they are "sounding brass, or a tinkling cymbal."

To the early Christians, the life beyond death seemed very close and very real. "What is a man profited," Jesus had asked, "if he shall gain the whole world, and lose his own soul?" This question placed the issue squarely before his followers: Did it not mean that the individual was of greater value than the whole world? The "otherworldliness" of the first Christians brought mankind to a high watermark of courage and compassion in both religious and secular history. The Romans, rulers of the known world, did not know what to make of them. Rome ruled by the threat of death. But here were people unaffected by that threat! The only effect of the massacres of Christians was to reveal their superior characters to the rest of the populace, hence to convert them to the new faith!

When the threat of death failed, there was nothing for the Romans to do but take over Christian Catholicism as the official state religion. Some historians have remarked that this act so reversed the nature of Christianity that it became more Roman than Catholic. This altered institution, after the fall of Rome, found its challenge in a very different kind of mission. Whereas it had been teaching religion to highly civilized peoples, its new role was to teach civilization to barbarians. Sometimes, during the terrible black centuries of the so-called Dark Ages, there seemed some question whether the barbarians would be ennobled by the church or the church degraded by the barbarians.

For our present purpose, we need not go into great detail concerning the beliefs of the various Celtic, Nordic, Frankish, and Germanic tribes that had broken the Roman power and were now asserting themselves. Though it is believed by some scholars that the Druids had advanced religious concepts, most of the tribes followed primitive nature worship. For churchmen and tribesmen alike, the Dark Ages are a dark story. Seldom has human conduct sunk below the level of those terrible 900 years. By the year 1000 most of Europe had been "converted"—at sword's point if necessary. The quality of conversions produced by such means had been questioned ever since. Through all these vicissitudes, however, man never surrendered his firm belief in the continuance of life in some form—usually, among the woods tribes, a happy hunting ground under the jurisdiction of a benevolent nature god.

At the beginning of the fourteenth century there burst upon the Western world the first rounded, inclusive, eloquent, inspired exposition of the purpose and structure of the life beyond death it had seen in more than a millennium. Though Dante's *Divine Comedy* was doubtless intended by its author to be as much a secular-philosophical poem as a religious treatise, it was from its first publication accorded the kind of awed respect traditionally only given to religious revelation. Dante Alighieri, born into the midst of the murderous political strife of his native Florence A.D. 1265, though the outstanding intellect of his day, found himself on the losing side of a political vendetta, exiled from his native city and forbidden to return on pain of being burned at the stake, an outcast without resources or reputation while still a young man. Dante, who on occasion spoke of himself as having visions and revelations, drew in broad outline from Aquinas, Aristotle, and Roman Catholic tradition for his description of "the state of the soul after death."

Dante was both a poetic and psychic visionary from youth. A passage from Giovanni C. Boccaccio's biography of the poet describes Dante's prophetic vision presaging the early death of the young Beatrice Portinari. This came upon him shortly after Dante first met the girl:

> In the Vita Nuova, he tells us that, having received a pleasant salutation from Beatrice Portinari, the young lady of his love, "I quitted the company, as it were, in a state of intoxication; and retiring to my

chamber, I sat down to meditate on this most courte-
ous lady. During my meditation a sweet sleep came
over me, in which appeared a wonderful vision. I
seemed to see in my chamber a cloud as red as fire, in
the midst of which I discerned the figure of a man
whose aspect struck fear into the beholder, whilst,
wonderful to say, he appeared all joy. He spoke of
many things, few of which I understood; but amongst
them was this, 'Ego dominus tuus,' 'I am thy master.'
In his arms I seemed to see a sleeping figure, naked,
except a slight covering of a blood-red colored drapery;
but looking more attentively, I saw that it was my lady
of happiness, who had condescended to address me on
the day before. In one of his hands he seemed to hold
something, which was all in flames, and to say these
words, 'Vide cor tuum,' 'Behold thy heart.'—And after
a short time he seemed to me to awaken her who slept,
and to exert his skill in such wise that he forced her
to eat that which was burning in his hand—and this
she did with hesitation and fear. He stayed but a short
time after this, but his joy was changed into a most
bitter lamentation. Weeping, he folded her in his
arms, and, with her, directed his course to heaven."

Dante went so far beyond anything his original sources
had revealed that his admirers consider *The Divine
Comedy* to be a genuine revelation. As a poetic device for
mounting his great description of the life beyond death,
Dante gives us a vision of himself, being on the point of
despair, being conducted, for the good of his soul,
through hell, purgatory, and paradise to the very light of
the presence of God. The poem is an allegory, with the
poet Vergil representing reason, a glorified female spirit

known as Beatrice representing revelation, and St. Bernard representing the intuitions of faith.

Dante's hell (Inferno) is a logical sort of place where the sin is its own punishment. The proud aristocrat Farinata, for example, burns for eons in the fierce flames of his own pride. The adulterous lovers, Paolo and Francesca, must live on locked in the inescapable bond of their own infatuation. The violent must continue for ages in acting out their own unrestrained violence and bestiality, and so on. The soul, guided by Vergil, goes deeper and deeper into hell as the crimes increase in seriousness—hypocrisy, cheating, theft, murder—until the adventurers reach the ugly, half-buried body of Satan at the very bottom of the pit. Climbing over Satan's body, they emerge on the other side and begin the upward climb through purgatory, where destructive habits may be left behind and new inspiration gained for the upward journey toward paradise. The seven circles of purgatory correspond with the seven deadly sins: pride, envy, anger, sloth, avarice, gluttony, and carnality. Purified souls, having passed through their purgatory, are led to the earthly paradise at the summit of purgatory. The soul has now reached the plane of earthly virtue but is still not qualified for the advanced reaches of paradise.

The soul's journey through paradise to heaven is symbolized by stops at various astronomical bodies—way stations where spirits in the realms of joy, but still short of heavenly perfection, gather. These represent the cardinal virtues—justice, prudence, temperance, fortitude—and the theological virtus—faith, hope, and charity. At last the soul, in ecstasy, reaches the heaven where all space is here and all time is now. No such summary as here given, of course, can reproduce the richness of thought, subtlety of meaning, and profundity of insight which have made Dante's description of the life beyond death a universally acknowledged masterpiece.

For the next systematized, inspired, and detailed account of the world beyond our earth plane, we go to eighteenth-century Sweden and the great scientist, philosopher, and seer Emanuel Swedenborg. The fact that several of my close friends are Swedenborgians—members of the church founded on Swedenborg's teachings—gives me a special pleasure in recounting this passage.

Emanuel was the son of a remarkable father, a bishop and professor of theology who was constantly in trouble with the religious authorities because he insisted that direct religious experience was more important than stale religious dogma. Emanuel was a brilliant scholar from boyhood and won a world reputation while still a young man. Late in life he wrote to a friend that his thirty-five years as a natural scientist were simply the Lord's preparation of him to receive the secrets of the life beyond death. His accomplishments as a scientist were phenomenal. He suggested the nebular hypothesis of the solar system—a great swirling mass condensed into sun and planets—long before Laplace and Kant. He made important discoveries perfecting our understanding of phosphorescence, magnetism, and atomic theory, as well as pioneered the science of crystallography. As an anatomist and physiologist he outlined the modern science of neurology, particularly in diagramming the functions of brain cells, cerebral cortex, and spinal cord. He antici-

pated later research in endrocrinology. Swedenborg did
not restrict himself to theoretical science but was an active participant in public affairs as a government official
and legislator. His scientific writings were in Latin.

Swedenborg, one of the great psychics of all time, was
experiencing spontaneous psychic phenomena even
while still engrossed in his studies of natural science. One
of the most clearly evidential cases of clairvoyance ever
known was demonstrated while he was visiting away from
home. One Saturday afternoon, while in Gothenburg, he
"saw" that Stockholm, 300 miles away, was burning. It
was the great Stockholm fire of 1759. His clairvoyant vision revealed to him that the fire spread rapidly, burned
the house of a friend, and was threatening his own Stockholm residence when, about 8 P.M., it was extinguished.
On Tuesday morning news of the fire reached Gothenburg from Stockholm; it had been exactly as Swedenborg
described it.

When he was fifty-seven years old, he was caught up in
a spiritual experience so overwhelming that it seemed
that the "heavens were opened" to him. He abandoned
his studies in natural science to explore these new dimensions of reality. He had, he said, free access to the world
of spirit, allowing him to move about it with complete
freedom, conversing with its inhabitants and exploring
its terrain. Though Swedenborg never preached or at-
tempted to found a sect—the Swedenborgian Church was
founded by admiring followers—he wrote extensively
about his travels in the farther world and published a
complete and detailed description.

At the ordinary levels of the after life, Swedenborg
matter-of-factly reports a world having much in common

with our own. He found a natural terrain and population centers containing men and women with all the habits and aspirations of familiar humanity. Everyone is
busy in some pursuit for the general good, and all are
both learning and teaching—learning from souls who
have gone to a higher wisdom, teaching the befuddled
and confused among the newly arrived. Swedenborg
thought that the universal human fear of death was
totally unnecessary. It was perfectly possible for enlightened humans to move comfortably and naturally
from one realm to the other. After transition, the body
falls. We find ourselves at ease in the midst of the spirit
world. Thus "heaven and earth might be together, and
might form one; men knowing what is in heaven, and
angels what is in the world."

Swedenborg scoffed at the notion that individuals
somehow become more noble just because they have
passed to the next sphere. "Our crochet of the abstract
nobleness of spirits," he wrote, "receives a rude shock.
Our father's souls are no better than ourselves; no less
mean and no less bodily, and their occupations are often
more unworthy than our own. A large part of their doings reads like police reports. Even the angels are but good
men in a favoring sphere; we may not worship them, for
they do not deserve it. At best they are of our brethren
the prophets. It is very matter of fact, death is no change
of substantials. The same problems recur after it, and
man is left to solve them. Nothing but goodness and
truth are thriving. There is no rest beyond the tomb, but
in the peace of God, which was rest before it."

Here, of course, he is speaking of the intermediate
realms of these newly arrived in the other sphere. More

advanced souls become aware of a central radiance, a spiritual light emanating from God, the source of strength, truth, love, and joy. Before these higher realms can be reached, the powerful undertow of the negative emotions—hatred, pride, attachment to appetites, habits, and possessions—must be overcome. A significant part of the work of an advanced soul is helping new arrivals in this struggle.

Madame Guyon, the French mystic of the seventeenth century, gave an account of communication in the afterworld which tallies very well with that given by my own control, Fletcher. Both authorities say that direct mind-to-mind communication soon replaces the cumbersome mechanisms of language. "There is," Madame Guyon wrote, "another manner of conversing than by speech. I learned then a language which before had been unknown to me. I gradually perceived, when Father Lacombe entered, that I could speak no more, and that there was formed in my soul the same kind of silence toward him as was formed in it with regards to God. I comprehended that God was willing to show me that men in this life might learn the language of angels. I was gradually reduced to speak to him only in silence. It was then that we understood each other in God, after a manner unutterable and all divine. We passed hours in this profound silence, always communicative, without uttering one word."

Swedenborg was the last great scientist of Western civilization to possess and demonstrate remarkable psychic powers. Many leading scientists have *acknowledged* psychic phenomena and insisted on their importance as pointers to the true nature of man. But none since

Swedenborg has both possessed such powers and been willing publicly to demonstrate them. (Numerous medical men of our own time have these powers but don't want it generally known for fear of damage to their professional reputations!) The reason may be found in the rationalized materialism that grew up within and finally took over almost completely what might be called "the official mind" of Western man. After Swedenborg came the steam engine, the spinning jenny, the power loom, the factory system, the Industrial revolution. An overwhelming tide of rational, materialistic skepticism confronted and threatened to engulf any who opposed its views. We are creatures of our times. To go through life regarded by most of one's contemporaries as a madman is no easy task. But who is really mad? Is it the person who insists that there is no reality except that which can be measured, weighed, heard and smelled, bought and sold? Or is it the person who, having discovered a range of dimensions not reached by the five gross senses, perceives a more expansive universe?

All through the Age of Reason, into the eighteenth-century Industrial Revolution, through the enormous exploitive expansion of nineteenth-century mechanical invention, and into the technological explosion of the twentieth century, with its automation and cybernation, Western man has wrung enormous material gains from the earth by applying himself single-mindedly to the manipulation of materials and excluding, so far as is possible, all other values. The history of Western philosophy from Hume, to Kant, to Comte, to Russell is a record of Western man's battle to preserve his transcendental

values against the rising tide of commercialized materialism.

The economic basis for the popular philosophies is
obvious. The governing elite was gaining money, prestige, and power by the rational manipulation of materials. Any principles, valid or not, that tended to curb
materialistic expansion had to be talked down and discredited. Those philosophers who most ardently supported the materialistic hypothesis found themselves in
control of the academic "city hall" of philosophy. Their
conclusions, if one took them seriously, would chill one's
bones. A few characteristic quotes from ranking philosophers of the materialist school: "Everything should be
explicable in terms of physics, including the behavior of
man. So far as science is concerned there is nothing in
the world but increasingly complex arrangements of
physical constituents." Another philosopher: "The relation between thought and the brain is roughly of the
same order as that between bile and the liver or urine
and the bladder." Another: " 'What is the explanation of
the universe?' is a senseless question." "It is impossible
for human beings to know whether there is a God or
not. The discussion is meaningless."

Fortunately, we have not been left without
philosophical antidotes for viewpoints, like those just
quoted, which do such violence to all that is beautiful
and exuberant in human, natural, and universal life.
One of them was William James, whose work will be discussed more fully in the next chapter. Another is that
body of high-level philosophical work contributed by
philosophers of equal or superior rank to those just

quoted, and flatly contradicting them. A third is evolution-of-consciousness theory, which fully explains how it can happen that events totally incomprehensible at one level of human consciousness are clearly and obviously perceptible at higher levels of awareness.

This latter strand of thought has been a prominent one in the twentieth century, supported by such eminent thinkers as Henri Bergson, C. G. Jung, Julian Huxley, P. B. Medawar, T. A. Goudge, Teilhard de Chardin and Erich Kahler. My favorite exposition of this philosophy is the one given by the Canadian psychiatrist R. M. Bucke. "The range of simple consciousness," says Bucke, "is far less than that of self-consciousness, and the range of cosmic consciousness is far greater than either. The man who has had the cosmic sense for even a few moments only will probably never again descend to the spiritual level of the merely self-conscious man, but will always feel within him the purifying, strengthening and exalting effect of that divine illumination, and many of those about him will recognize that his spiritual stature is above that of the average man."

Lower levels of consciousness, unable to comprehend dimensions which are clear at the higher levels, naturally must protest that such dimensions do not exist. There is the reported incident of a bulldozer operator who was confronted by a group of embattled environmentalists as he was about to destroy one of the beauty spots of an eastern suburb. The bulldozer jockey placed his hands on his hips, spat on the ground, and looked around him. "What beauty?" he said. "I don't see no beauty." Who, in this instance, is to be believed: the mechanic who could see no beauty or the environmentalists who could?

In this age-old controversy, I take comfort in the wry good humor with which the matter is disposed of by a man rated in standard textbooks of philosophy as one of the outstanding philosophical giants of our time, C. D. Broad, Knightsbridge Professor of Philosophy in Cambridge University. The Cambridge sage has addressed himself to the contention, postulated by Bertrand Russell, Sigmund Freud, and others, that all religious experiences are of the same nature as illusions and hallucinations. ("From a scientific point of view," Russell said, "we can make no distinction between the man who eats little and sees heaven and the man who drinks much and sees snakes.") Professor Broad good-naturedly goes along with the possibility that the travelers in the larger dimensions may seem a little odd:

> Suppose, for the sake of argument, that there is an aspect of the world which remains altogether outside the ken of ordinary persons in their daily life. Then it seems very likely that some degree of mental and physical abnormality would be a necessary condition for getting sufficiently loosened from the objects of ordinary sense perception to come into cognitive contact with this aspect of reality. Therefore the fact that those persons who claim to have this peculiar kind of cognition generally exhibit certain mental and physical abnormalities is rather what might be anticipated if their claims were true. One might need to be slightly "cracked" in order to have some peepholes into the supersensible world.

But Professor Broad does not believe that the Freudians and Professor Russell are right. "Their theories," he writes, "wear too jaundiced a complexion to inspire complete confidence. I should feel some hesitation in accepting theories about the nature of music and its function in human life, excogitated by a tone-deaf psychologist whose wife had recently eloped with a musician."

IV

Survival Insights: William James
and the Pioneer Researchers

AN ECOLOGIST FRIEND of mine, much upset about
the destruction of our natural environment, once said to
me, "There is only one thing preventing clean air, pure
drinking water, healthy streams, productive soil, and un-
polluted food—a failure to believe that these things can
be had. The moment we believe such a world to be ob-
tainable, and worth attaining, we will quickly create it."

I have often thought that something similar applies to
our failure to abolish our fear of death by an openminded consideration of the possibilities of a progression
to an exciting and fulfilling life in another sphere. In the
fact of an almost palpable will-not-to-believe, evidence
means nothing and is not even seriously considered.

Is it possible that this will-not-to-believe may have an
effect similar to our will-not-to-preserve, as applied to our
natural environment? It is my conviction that the life
after death is a reality for those who believe in it and for
those who do not. I am convinced that leaving one's

mind open to the creative possibilities of such a life will add greatly to the enjoyment and ultimate meaning of that life when it comes—as it does to about 50,000,000 people each year, and does, inevitably, for each of us. This chapter is partly devoted to what might be called the power of institutionalized disbelief and to some of those who have most effectively dealt with it.

What is the human brain?

This question has not found an answer on which leading authorities can agree, though it is acknowledged to be one of the most important ones ever asked by man and accordingly has engaged the best minds of the twentieth century.

Is it, as some say, an organ of secretion, producing consciousness as liver produces bile? In this case, of course, since dead livers produce no bile, consciousness would end when the brain stopped functioning.

Or is it, as many scientists and philosophers of science insist, an organ more fittingly compared with the lungs, taking from an all-embracing awareness that minute-to-minute measure of consciousness needed to sustain a given psyche through its immediate universe situation— just as the lungs draw from a vast surrounding atmosphere that measure of oxygen necessary to sustain a physical body in its moment-to-moment world needs? In this case the individual psyche, once formed into a structure of consciousness (as a physical body is formed of a structure of atoms) would be existing in its own element and would be deprived of nothing essential to its existence of a brain ceased transmitting data to it.

These two points of view have never been resolved. Mechanistic scientists, like the man in the street, find their services so engaged in profitable activity in the "practical" activities of their day that they will not examine evidence that casts doubt on the mechanistic universe and the "liver" theory of the brain. Cosmic-consciousness scientists find the evidence for the mental universe and the "lungs" theory of the brain so overwhelming that even though the temporary scientific fad is to allow them no hearing and punish them, whenever possible, with reduced professional status, they cannot in honesty abandon their case.

The importance of this issue to the present discussion is clear. If human personality ends when the brain no longer works, there need be no speculation about an afterlife. If, however, the brain is a "consciousness pump," impelling into a temporary organism such little jets of cosmic awareness as can be utilized by a growing consciousness unit within a physical organism—and at the same time feeding local physical sense data into that same temporary psychosomatic system—there is no need for a brain once the psyche has grown strong enough to subsist in its own element. One does not need a water-supply system, with its complicated arrangement of pumps, pipes, valves, and spigots, when one is swimming in a stream of pure water.

A number of superb minds have seen that in the successful understanding of the cosmic function of the human brain lies the very future of man. In mechanism (since this approach is the current conventional wisdom and known to every seventh-grader, there is no need to develop it here) they see a disastrous dead end, with man endlessly and blindly fumbling with molecules until at last he blows himself up with them. In cosmic consciousness they see reflected the clear meaning of aspects of human experience now unexplained—and a fruitful rebirth of scientific inquiry on an enormously expanded horizon.

One of the greatest of these minds—the pioneer, the groundbreaker, the great far-ranging mental explorer who pointed to realms later investigated in greater detail by such giants as Jung, Dewey, and Freud—was William James. Since James was a leader in building the bridge of comprehension by which rational certainty and intuited mystery may live comfortably—even joyously—within the same world concept, we must consider the main points of his thought before we can fully appreciate the most recent experiences of the life beyond death.

Today's standard psychology texts cite William James as one of the four founders of modern psychology, the others being Wilhelm Wundt, John Dewey, and Sigmund Freud. Each of these pioneers utilized the work of the others—Wundt contributing the experimental techniques which dominate present-day psychological research, James the concept of studying the human personality as a functioning whole, Freud the techniques of psychoanalysis by free association, Dewey the concept of mental activity as an evolutionary solving of problems growing out of direct human experience.

James never denied the unquestioned fact that much of human activity is made up of simple, machinelike automatisms. Indeed, his functionalism is the basis for today's understanding and curing of such functional neuroses as deafness to avoid hearing unwelcome sounds, blindness to avert distasteful sights, gluttony and kleptomania to compensate for a shortage of love, powerdriving to cover a sense of inadequacy, and so on. It is also the basis for his conviction that human consciousness is much more than a network of stimulus-response cycles. His direct observation of human mental and physical behavior led him to seek the function of which the event was a by-product. He was convinced that a thorough understanding of man the machine was essential to a full understanding of man. His studies in mental functionalism disposed of many false notions about God and immortality.

But these same studies led him to the discovery of higher functions within man which are not accounted for by any of the earthbound mechanistic theories. Of the four founders of modern psychology, only James and Freud showed any awareness of the vast reverberating overtones beyond the clinical circuits that had so fascinated them all. Freud became aware of these overtones too late in his life (not long before his death he wrote that if he had had it all to do over again, he would have been a parapsychologist) to have any effect on the flourishing school of psychology that bears his name. James, however, noted the significant variations while still in his professional prime. To James, it was obvious that the value of any hypothesis is inversely proportional to the range of human experience it leaves unexplained. He wrote extensively about the phenomena that continually occur quite outside the guidelines of mechanistic psychology and laid the groundwork for a careful study of these events. For this reason, if our aim is to bring under the purview of scientific study the full range of actual occurrences within the experience of man, we must return to the foundation left by William

James and the insights the later Freudians so conspic-uously missed.

William James brought an extraordinary range of ex-perience to the studies that led to his final pronounce-ments on the question of the life beyond death. He was one of the five children of a brilliant, restless, wandering father. Henry James the elder (the novelist Henry James was one of his sons and a brother of William) was the scion of a long line of prosperous Scotch-Irish-English Presbyterian farmers, traders, and merchants. As a young man the senior James had been sent to Princeton Theological Seminary, where he developed a furious aversion to organized religion. He later wrote extensively and brilliantly on philosophical and theological topics and was a close friend of such intellectual leaders of his time as Emerson and Carlyle. Because of his father's in-nate tendency to rove, William's education was con-ducted on two continents and often interrupted. As a boy, William attended various schools in the United States, France, and Switzerland. At eighteen he took up the study of art, only to abandon it and enroll the following year in the Lawrence Scientific School of Har-vard University. He went on to graduate, after several in-terruptions, from the Harvard Medical School. One of these interruptions was an exploration of the Amazon Valley as assistant to the great scientist Louis Agassiz. An-other was an interlude in Germany to study under the famous scientist Hermann von Helmholtz.

James' physical health was precarious throughout his adolescence. Bouts of illness from time to time confined him to bed, where his thoughts turned introspective and sometimes even suicidal. It was here, perhaps, that he developed that extraordinary sympathy for and understanding of mental illness and suffering that was a feature of all his later works. These depressions ended abruptly when, at the age of twenty-eight, he discovered the work of the French philosopher Charles B. Renouvier. The great French thinker argued that the distinguishing feature of the human being is not his automatism but his unceasing drive toward ever greater freedom of thought and action through the exercise of that limited faculty which he, alone of all the creatures, possesses—free will. To the young William James, it was a revelation. "My first act of free will," he wrote, "will be to believe in free will." This resolve released his pent-up creativity. He was married not long thereafter and, with an energy and brilliance rarely seen in any human being, set out on the far-ranging investigations which were to bring him lasting renown.

He progressed from one subject to another, making notable original contributions at each stop, always utilizing previously acquired knowledge as a point of departure for further inquiry. First he became a professor of physiology at Harvard. He then became a professor of psychology and crowned this phase of his career with the great two-volume *Principles of Psychology*. This work, appearing in 1890, was immediately recognized in world centers of learning as an epoch-making new departure. It overthrew the established curricula in "mental science" and permanently established the functional point of view in psychology. It was a period of swift advance in the understanding of the mundane activities of the human mind. Josef Breuer, in Germany had, in 1880, using hypnosis, cured a patient of a mental illness

brought on by a buried traumatic experience. This had
attracted the interest of young Dr. Sigmund Freud, who,
working with Breuer, was about to bring out the first
book on psychoanalytic therapy. With his own discoveries and his keen and sympathetic awareness of the work
of Wundt, Breuer, and Freud, James for the rest of his
life rode the front edge of the wave of psychological advance.

James discovered in middle age, after having risen to
the very pinnacle of world achievement in his chosen
field of psychology, that this field contained limitations
preventing a full comprehension of the nature and destiny of man. Psychology correctly concentrated on a careful study of man as he is, to help him solve his immediate
and local problems and, if possible, relieve his mental
symptoms. James found these boundaries hampering in
many ways. They precluded any mention of man's cosmic
origin, function, and ultimate purpose. They elevated
the laboratory cast of mind and the myth of objectivity to
a status above other modes of perception which it was
highly questionable that they deserved. So, while retain-
ing and utilizing to the utmost the insights he had gained
through his psychological researches, he abandoned psychology as a "little" science. He now carried its basic insights over into the field of philosophy, where, he felt,
the search for ultimate truth would find a freer range.
His method—the resting of any claim to knowledge
solely on the foundation of direct human experience—
was the same as that he had used in psychology and was
equally successful. He was neither arguing foregone conclusions nor carrying these conclusions into further
dialectic. In approaching the formidable questions of

God and immortality, he appealed not to authority, theory, or skilled argumentation, but to what had actually happened to living human beings. James could not commit himself hastily. It was ten years—during which time he published cautious essays reporting his painstaking investigations along these lines—before he reached any but tentative conclusions, and even these were hedged with admonitions that a great deal of confirmatory work still needed to be done.

In the end, he was completely convinced of the existence of God. It is doubtful, of course, whether his definition of God would have suited the requirements of the ranking clergymen of his time. But he believed it to have been established beyond any possible question that there existed saving powers, psychic and spiritual in nature, with which one's personality could make contact in crisis. Because the fact of telepathy—thought transference—had now been established, he found the question of immortality to be far more difficult and complex. To establish the kind of proof of survival that would satisfy the most exacting skeptic (James fully sympathized with the skeptical point of view and maintained its strictures throughout his investigations) one would have to present evidence that could not be explained by any conceivable transference of any conceivable human thoughts in the minds (conscious or unconscious) of any living human beings.

Time after time he found cases in which explanation by telepathy hypothesis seemed far more preposterous than explanation by survival hypothesis. Yet so long as the telepathy hypothesis could be tolerated at all, he could not feel that the case was *scientifically* conclusive.

That it was logically and morally conclusive he had no question.

An opportunity for James to organize and present his thinking and research on these questions presented itself when, in 1902, he was invited to deliver the Gifford Lectures at the University of Edinburgh. These twenty lectures, published in book form as the *Varieties of Religious Experience,* presented the general line of thought on the life beyond death to which he adhered for the rest of his life. They have sometimes been equaled, but never surpassed, in their cogent welding of man's spiritual and scientific experience. "It is worth remembering," Columbia University's famous scholar Jacques Barzun wrote in a 1958 evaluation of the book, "that James had come to philosophy from psychology—his classic treatise of 1890 being to this day a landmark in the history of that science. Before being a psychologist, James had been trained as chemist and a physician, so that his evolution from the study of matter to the study of man's religious longings was throughout supported by science, which was the kind of knowledge this century most admired."

To quote any particular passage of a work as rich and profound as the *Varieties* is to risk committing the crime of distortion; one really must read it all. Nevertheless, I must run this risk. One passage, during James' discussion of attitudes toward religion, has long been one of my favorites:

> There is a state of mind, known to religious men, but to no others, in which the will to assert ourselves and hold our own has been displaced by a willingness to close our mouths and be as nothing in the floods

and waterspouts of God. In this state of mind, what we most dreaded has become the habitation of our safety, and the hour of our moral death has turned into our spiritual birthday. But time for tension in our soul is over, and that of happy relaxation . . . in an eternal present, with no discordant future to be anxious about, has arrived. . . . We shall see how infinitely passionate a thing religion at its highest flights can be. Like love, like wrath, like hope, ambition, jealousy, like every other instinctive eagerness and impulse, it adds to life an enchantment which is not rationally or logically deducible from anything else. . . . If religion is to mean anything definite for us, it seems to me that we ought to take it as meaning this added dimension of emotion, this enthusiastic temper of espousal, in regions where morality strictly so called can at best but bow its head and acquiesce. It ought to mean nothing short of this new reach of freedom for us, with the struggle over, the keynote of the universe sounding in our ears, and everlasting possession spread before our eyes. . . . There are plenty of sombre religious men in whom this rapturous message is lacking . . . yet it is religion in the acutest, most passionate sense that I wish, without disputing about words, to study first. . . . There are saints who have grown in happiness just in proportion as their outward state grew more intolerable. No other emotion than religious emotion can bring a man to this peculiar pass. I think we ought to look for the answer among these violenter examples rather than among those of a more moderate hue.

Of course, not all of William James' pronouncements are so lyrical. He speaks from a background as anatomist and laboratory psychologist. A remark more typical of him can be found in his Harvard lecture on immortality. Here he concedes without question that thought is a function of the brain. He does not see that this fact in any way interferes with the likelihood of immortality. "Even though our soul's life, as we now understand it, may be in literal strictness the function of a brain that perishes, yet it is not at all impossible, but on the contrary quite possible, that the life may still continue when the brain itself is dead." He goes on to explain that nature provides many examples of a productive function being combined with other functions. "The trigger of a cross-bow has a releasing function; it removes the obstacle holding the string and lets the bow fly back to its original shape. . . . The keys of an organ open various pipes and let the wind in the air chest escape in various ways. . . . We are not required to think only of the brain's productive function; we are entitled also to consider its transmissive function." He then suggests that our brains could be half-transparent lenses through which the white radiance of reality is colored by the nature of the individual lens. "Our consciousness as we here know it would in literal strictness be the function of the brain. . . . But such dependence on the brain for this natural life would in no wise make immortal life impossible. . . . In strict logic then, the fangs of cerebralistic materialism are drawn . . . you may henceforth believe in immortality, whether you care to profit by the permission or not." I have always taken this as an invitation to use our brain-generated intelligence to invite an enlarged consciousness rather than to shut it out.

In most of William James' writing he is much more the down-to-earth researcher. He stated his final position on human immortality in an article which was published in the *American Magazine* less than a year before his death. Here he touches some of the highlights of his quarter century of experience as a psychical researcher. "I wish to go on record," he wrote, "for the *commonness* of these phenomena. . . . I am constantly baffled as to what to think of this or that particular story, for the sources of error in any one observation are seldom fully knowable. But weak sticks make strong faggots, and when the stories fall into consistent sorts that point each in a definite direction, one gets a sense of being in the presence of . . . genuine phenomena."

He affirmed the undoubted presence of an authentic will to communicate. "As to there being such real natural types of psychic phenomena, ignored by orthodox science, I am not baffled at all, for I am fully convinced of it." Nothing in this final pronouncement changes the stand he had taken in *Varieties* ten years earlier; he reiterated the difficulty of distinguishing between living-telepathic and discarnate-spirit communication and encouraged greatly increased research: "it is eminently a case for facts to testify."

He then referred his readers to the most important work then in progress in this area: "I have the highest respect for the patient labors of Messrs. Myers, Hodgson and Hyslop." In carrying out the task of this chapter, which is to help adjust our materialistic-scientific-conditioned minds, using the usual language of science, to possibilities science has not yet fully inquired into, there seems to be no better course than to follow William James' advice and consider these landmarks in psychical research.

James Hyslop was a Columbia University professor who became one of the founders of the American Society for Psychical Research in 1906. Before his death in 1920, he had greatly advanced our techniques of psychical research and shed important new light on our understanding of psychic phenomena. Dr. Richard Hodgson was one of the members of the British Society for Psychical Research known for his ruthless exposure of fraud, his unrelenting skepticism, and his insistence that if the scientific world were to be convinced, the most meticulous care would have to be taken with everything reported as fact. Hodgson was for a time in charge of the American branch of the British SPR; when he died (1905), this branch became the nucleus of the new American SPR. The contributions of Frederic Myers, particularly his extensive explorations of the conditions of the life after death, are so vast they will require a separate chapter. Here we need only note that Myers, essayist and classical scholar at Cambridge, was a founding member and past president of the British SPR.

Other members of this great pioneering research organization will turn up later in our travels in that other sphere, so we may as well introduce them now. These are of particular importance: Henry Sidgwick, a professor of philosophy at Cambridge and first president of the BSPR; Edmund Gurney, professor of psychology at Cambridge and a BSPR past president; Arthur Conan Doyle, a British physician who turned author and became world-famous as the creator of Sherlock Holmes; and Oliver Lodge, one of England's most distinguished physicists, who had been knighted for his outstanding work in atomic and electrical theory. It was through the heartrending loss of Lodge's son Raymond, at the very time when Sir Oliver was immersed in the most intensive phase of his psychical research, that science received its first detailed account of the twentieth century describing the experience of the entry into and firm establishment within the world beyond death.

In Sir Oliver Lodge's book about these extraordinary communications, *Raymond,* and in subsequent analyses and evaluations by SPR authorities, much space is given to the technicalities of psychical research. Precisely which words gave incontrovertible proof that the communicator was Lodge's son Raymond and no one else? To what extent were the communications "contaminated" by telepathic, mediumistic, and other influences? Is it probable that Raymond was in a half-asleep dream state in some cases and fully awake in others? Since Raymond was not a trained scientist, his descriptions would have to be purely impressionistic; what scientific conclusions about the underlying structures and energies of the afterworld could be drawn from his impressions?

All these matters are, of course, of vital importance to the scientists. They will come up again in a later passage in this book. For now, I would like to attend mainly to the experience itself—what does the entry into that other world actually *feel* like? In this quality of spontaneous, subjective expression of direct experience, I regard the Raymond communications as almost perfectly "pure"— that is, free from contaminations—possessing a definite value for those of us who are more inclined to experience life than to analyze it. I will, therefore, in the following account, dispense with the technical comments of the psychical researcher and let Raymond "come through."

Raymond Lodge, a junior British officer in France during World War I, was killed in action in September, 1915. At this time his father, Sir Oliver Lodge, in the normal course of the psychical researches which were now taking up most of his time, was working anonymously—that is, without the mediums' knowing his true identity—with three mediums: Mrs. Katharine Kennedy, an automatist (automatic trance-writer); Mrs. Gladys Osborne Leonard, who worked both in trance and through table tilting, but mainly, in these communications, in trance; and Mr. A. Vout Peters, a trance medium. At this time—and, as we shall see, later—it was not unusual for Frederic Myers, who had died in 1901 and was now most active in the discarnate world, to talk, through mediums, with his earth-side friends. The first foreshadowing of Raymond's death came in a communication from Myers known as the "Faunus" message.

Raymond Lodge was killed in Flanders on September 14, 1915; he was then in his twenty-sixth year. On August 8, 1915—more than a month before Raymond's death—in a sitting with the famous American medium Mrs. Lenore Piper in Greenfield, Massachusetts, a brief message from Myers to Lodge was noted. This was routinely sent to Lodge as part of the international network of correspondence the psychical researchers of the time had set up. Dr. Richard Hodgson (died 1905) was speaking through the medium. This was his message: "Now, Lodge, while we are not here as of old, that is not quite, we are here enough to take and give messages. Myers says you take the part of the poet, and he will act as Faunus. Faunus. Verrall will understand."

It was well known by this time that Myers, who had been an eminent classical scholar earth-side, often gave his messages in the form of allusions to Greek and Roman poetry and other classical works—an area of scholarship almost certain to be unknown to the average medium and hence free from "contamination"—to establish his identity beyond question. "Verrall" referred to Mrs. Arthur W. Verrall, widow of a distinguished Cambridge classical scholar and an accomplished classicist in her own right. She at once identified the passage and established its meaning. In the *Odes* of the Roman poet Horace there is an episode in which the poet is protected from harm from a falling tree by the god Faunus, "guardian of poets." This was interpreted to mean that Lodge was about to receive some kind of blow and that Myers would do what he could in the role of guardian.

Sir Oliver Lodge was helped in his psychical research by his entire family. The first séance attended by any member of the family after Raymond's death was held on September 25—eleven days after Raymond was killed. It was an anonymous table-tilting séance of Mrs. Lodge with Mrs. Leonard. The medium did not at this time know the correct identity of her sitter. No attempt was made to get in touch with Raymond. Nevertheless, the following message came through from the "dead" son: "Tell Father I have met some friends of his." Mrs. Lodge then asked if he could give a specific name. The answer came: "Yes, Myers." Two days later Sir Oliver had an anonymous trance sitting with the same medium. In this sitting, Mrs. Leonard's control, "Feda," announcing that Raymond was with her, spoke as follows: "He finds it difficult, he says, but he has got so many kind friends helping him. . . . He knows that as soon as he is a little more ready he has got a great deal of work to do. 'I almost wonder,' he says, 'shall I be fit and able to do it. They tell me I shall.' 'I have instructors and teachers with me.' He shows me the letter M. . . . I feel I have got two fathers now. . . . My old one, and another too. . . . There is a weight gone off his mind the last day or two; he feels brighter and lighter and happier altogether, the last few days. There was confusion at first. He could not get his bearings. . . . 'But I was not very long,' he says, 'and I think I was very fortunate; it was not very long before it was explained to me where I was.' "

On the same day, Mrs. Lodge had an anonymous trance sitting with Mr. Peters. The following message came through: "This gentleman who wrote poetry—I see the letter *M*—is helping your son to communicate." Shortly thereafter Peters jumped up in his chair, snapped his fingers and almost shouted: "Good God! How father will be able to see now! Much firmer than he has ever done, because it will touch our hearts." Two weeks later, at a table sitting with Mrs. Leonard, Myers confirmed the intent of the "Faunus" message as a promise of help to Raymond and his family during the transition. Two days later, on October 29, Lodge had a trance sitting with Peters in which Myers' "guardianship" of Raymond was again stressed: "Your common-sense method of approaching the subject in the family has been the means of helping Raymond to come back . . . without this is would have been far more difficult . . . he says to me: 'F. M. has helped me so much, more than you think' . . . then he says, 'For God's sake, father, break away the dam that people have set up. If you could only see what I see:

hundreds of men and women heart-broken. If you could only see the boys on our side shut out, you would throw the whole strength of yourself into this work.' . . . He wants me to tell you the feeling on going over was one of intense disappointment, he had no idea of death. The second too was grief . . . this is a time when men and woman have had the crust broken off them—a crust of convention, of . . . indifference, has been smashed, and everybody thinks, though some selfishly."

From here on, Raymond's course is one of gradual recovery, as from traumatic shock. There was full awareness of the opportunities of his situation and a vigorous eagerness to get on with them. The recovery, though slow, showed a steady, day-to-day, week-by-week improvement. During the sittings of this recovery period a question often asked on our side—"Do people in the afterlife ever sleep?"—received at least a partial answer. Raymond had met a young man named Paul who was helping him in his orientation. Their relationship was described in the automatic writing of Mrs. Kennedy: "Will you tell them that Raymond had been to you and that Paul tells me I can come too, whenever I like? . . . Paul tells me he has been here since he was seventeen; he is a jolly chap; everyone seems fond of him. . . . It seems a rule here to call Paul if you get in a fix." At this point Paul cut in: "Raymond has slept ever since last night." Paul then spoke of the general disappointment of persons newly arrived on his side on discovering how hard it was to get through to their friends and families that they still lived: "They hardly believe it yet that they have spoken. All the time they felt it was impossible, and they nearly gave it up, but I kept on begging them to tell

their mother they lived. . . . Such a lot of people think
their loved ones are dead. It is revolting to hear the boys
tell you how no one speaks to them ever."

At another recovery-period sitting, Feda, Mrs. Leonard's control, reported, "Raymond has not completely
learned how to build up as yet." He still "finds it difficult,
but has so many kind friends helping him." He knows
that "as soon as he is a little more ready, he has a great
deal of work to do."

By the middle of November, two months after his
death, Raymond is in full possession of his faculties, at
home in his new surroundings and fully able to describe
them in detail. He is far more sure of himself in handling
the difficult communication problems in getting messages
through to earth-side minds through mediums. Here he
gives us a strongly personal, subjective, impressionistic
account of how things look and feel *to him,* without the
complex analysis of whether his world is wholly mental,
quasi-physical, real or dream, and the other considerations so dear to the hearts of psychical researchers. He
simply tells, in a sitting with Mrs. Leonard, what he sees
and feels:

At first, there is some confused dialogue about arrangements on the other side. Then, after the remark "Prayer
helps when things are not relevant," things settle down
and Raymond is able to come through without further
interruption: "You [referring to the sitters] do not feel
so real as people do where he is, and walls appear transparent to him now. The great thing that made him rec-
onciled to his new surroundings was that things appear
so solid and substantial. . . . The first person to meet
him was Grandfather. And others then, some of whom he

had only heard about. They all appeared to be so solid, that he could scarcely believe that he had passed over. He lives in a house—a house built of bricks—and there are trees and flowers, and the ground is solid. . . . The night doesn't follow the day here, as it did on the earth-plane. It seems to get dark sometimes, when he would like it to be dark, but the time in between light and dark is not always the same. . . . What I am worrying around about is, how it's made, of what it is composed. I have not found out yet . . . for a little time I thought one's thoughts formed the buildings and the flowers and trees and solid ground; but there is more than that. . . . The greatest amount of his work is helping on poor chaps literally shot into the spirit world, at the war." When asked whether Raymond could see ahead, the reply came: "He thinks sometimes that he can, but it's not easy to predict. I don't think that I really know any more than when on earth."

At the next sitting with the same medium a few days later the combination of first- and third-person reporting is less in evidence, and Raymond comes through even more strongly as speaking in the first person and for himself: "If I come there must be no sadness. I don't want to be a ghost at the feast. There mustn't be one sigh. . . ." Asked about clothing, Raymond said, "They are all manufactured. Can you fancy you see me in white robes? Mind I didn't care for them at first, and I wouldn't wear them. Just like a fellow gone to a country where there is a hot climate—an ignorant fellow, not knowing what he was going to; it's just like that. He may make up his mind to wear his own clothes a little while, but he will soon be dressing like the natives. He was allowed to have earth clothes here until he got acclimatized; they let him; they didn't force him. I don't think I will ever be able to make the boys see me in white robes." At a later sitting, Raymond discussed his new body: "My body is very similar to the one I had before. I pinch myself sometimes to see if it's real and it is, but it doesn't seem to hurt as much as when I pinched the flesh body. The internal organs don't seem constituted on the same lines as before. They can't be quite the same but to all appearances, and outwardly, they are the same as before. I can move somewhat more freely."

Then the dialogue abruptly switches to third person: "Yes, he has eyelashes and eyebrows, exactly the same, and a tongue and teeth. He has got a new tooth now in place of another one he had—one that wasn't quite right then. He has got it right and a good tooth has come in place of the one that had gone. He knew a man who had lost his arm, but he has got another one. Yes, he has got two arms now. He seemed as if without a limb when first he entered the astral, seemed incomplete, but after a while it got more and more complete, until he got a new one. . . . When anybody's blown to pieces, it takes some time for the spirit-body to complete itself, to gather itself all in, and to be complete. It dissipated a certain amount of substance which is undoubtedly etheric, and it has to be concentrated again. The *spirit* isn't blown apart, of course, but it has an effect upon it. . . . Bodies should not be burned on purpose. We have terrible troubles sometimes over people who are cremated too soon . . . the idea seems to be 'hurry up and get them out of the way now that they are dead.' Not until seven days. . . ."

Then: "I don't think men and women stand to each

other quite the same as they did on the earth plane, but they seem to have the same feelings to each other, with a different expression of it. There don't seem to be any children born here. People are sent into the physical body to have children on the earth plane; they don't have them here. . . . He doesn't want to eat now but he sees some who do; he says they have to be given something which has all the appearance of an earth food. A chap came over the other day, who *would* have a cigar. 'That's finished them,' he thought . . . but they were able to manufacture what looked like a cigar . . . he had four altogether and now doesn't look at one. They don't seem to get the same satisfaction out of it, so gradually it seems to drop from them. But when they first come they do want things. Some want meat, and some strong drink. . . ." Raymond can see sun and stars but doesn't feel heat or cold. "That is not because the sun has lost its heat, but because he hasn't got the same body that sensed the heat. When he comes into contact with the earth plane, and is manifesting, then he feels a little cold or warm—at least he does when a medium is present—not when he comes in the ordinary way just to look around."

There follows some discussion of what kind of proof Raymond could provide that would be most evidential. The dialogue again goes to third person: "That's why he has been collecting information. He does so want to encourage people to look forward to a life they will certainly have to enter upon, and realize that it is a rational life." Then to first person: "I want to study things here a lot. Would you think it selfish if I say I wouldn't like to be back now?—I wouldn't give this up for anything." Persons much attached to their pets will be interested to know that a dog was seen—evidently the same dog, a bitch called Curly, mentioned some years previously, through another medium, by Myers.

From here on, after a mention of "hundreds of things I think of to tell you about when I am away from the medium," Raymond concentrates on giving evidence, sometimes through cross correspondences by two mediums, of knowledge concerning circumstances, family arrangements, pets, habits, and properties that only he could know, by way of establishing beyond any possible doubt that the entity communicating is indeed Raymond Lodge. After that, as in so many cases, the urgency and content of the information dwindle. One almost has a feeling that the communicator has had enough of being a dutiful son helping with his father's work and now would like to be about his own affairs. Before ending his communications, Raymond makes the interesting literary observation that books have already been prepared on his plane, awaiting an opportunity to be inserted into the minds of congenial authors and ultimately published on earth.

Sir Oliver Lodge has some pointed advice for bereaved persons at the close of his book *Raymond*: "It may be asked, do I recommend all bereaved persons to devote the time and attention which I have done to getting communications and recording them? Most certainly I do not. I am a student on the subject, and a student often undertakes detailed labor of a special kind. I recommend people in general to learn and realize that their loved ones are still active and useful and interested and happy —more alive than ever in one sense—and to make up their minds to live a useful life until they rejoin them."

All the great leaders of the British Society for Psychical Research—Sidgwick, Guerney, Myers, Hodgson—continued their psychical research, after their deaths, from the other side. They frequently appeared in séances with evidential material or helpful technical pointers. Of those mentioned by Professor James—Myers, Hodgson, and the brilliant American Hyslop—only Myers undertook a full description of the ever-expanding world beyond the earth life. Hodgson, however, elucidated the means by which discarnate persons are able to identify, then utilize available mediums. Hyslop left some instructive conclusions about the reality structure of the afterlife, made especially valuable by the enormous range of his research and observation.

In the opinion of Lodge, a very careful scholar, Hodgson made two vital contributions without which the whole project of psychical research could have made no further significant progress. Hodgson early recognized the importance of these problems and devoted years of his life to their solution. First, he identified the methods of trance communication and automatic writing and proved the correctness of his hypothesis by demonstration. Second, he developed material that abolished once and for all the hypothesis that all mediumistic communication was based on the medium's ability to extract information telepathically from the minds of living persons. This elimination of the telepathy-of-the-living theory left without challenge the fact of communication from persons presumed to be dead.

We all have bodies variously called ethereal or astral associated with our physical bodies. In the case of gifted mediums, said Dr. Hodgson, special stores of a peculiar kind of energy exists, and are visible to persons in the ethereal realm as "light." Mrs. Piper, the medium most closely studied by Hodgson, had two masses of it, one connected with her head, the other with her right arm and hand. "I do not profess," said Dr. Hodgson, "to be able to give any satisfactory explanation of the process I describe." That the process was actually in effect he demonstrated by arranging a sitting in which one discarnate personality communicated verbally, utilizing the "head energy," while another personality independently communicated a separate and coherent series of messages through the medium's arm and hand in automatic writing.

Hodgson's demolition of the telepathy-between-the-living notion included an able marshaling of the immense body of material that demonstrably could not have come from living minds. He also made some very original observations of his own. He made very careful notes of patterns of confusion, vagueness, fatigue, automatic repetition, and fading in séance experience. He made a very strong case, too complicated to repeat in our present context, for the possibility that the discarnate individual, in order to utilize the medium, would have to put himself into a dreamy, reminiscent state which would inhibit the use of full consciousness. He also pointed out the difficulty of a person who had put in a great many years trying to learn to use effectively one physical machine (his own), then obliged to learn entirely new living techniques without any physical machine at all, then thrown into a situation where he must try to manage an entirely unfamiliar physical mechanism. The actual results are exactly what one would expect of such a situation—one becomes more expert the longer one is at it. Hodgson showed again and again that treating his séance communicators as rational discarnate spirits operating under these difficulties produced far better results than treating the material as if it were telepathic impressions from living minds. He also noted the clearness of remembrance in little children recently deceased as contrasted with the forgetting of childish things shown by communicators who passed over as children long before. This is what one might expect of a normally developing, though discarnate person.

Professor Hyslop addressed himself to the theoretical problem of what the experienced world beyond is made of. Acknowledging that it is not of the same atomic, molecular, ionized, corpuscular, and electromagnetic stuff as the world of earth experience, there remain several possibilities of what it might be. There is much to suggest, he said, that the spiritual life after death is not based on sensory response to stimulus, but is mental and creative. Agreeing that a spiritual life demands that we get rid of the sensory life of appetites, this leaves us with our internal mental faculties as our basic equipment. "It is the inner life that survives," he wrote, "and not the physical."

Since the inner life is so largely made up of remembered sense experience, imprinted automatisms, and repetitive, conditioned thought habit, some of this must go along with us for the first part of the journey. Such a mind, it is reasonable to assume, would have to hallucinate for itself a reasonably livable facsimile of the old sense world as a temporary expedient while accustoming itself to the realities of living in a universe of pure mind and pure spirit. This mentally created world would seem very real to the individual—"very solid," as Raymond put it. The kindly society at the receiving end of the discarnate world, not wishing to upset the newly arrived spirit but, trying to help it in its development, would recognize this temporary need, encourage it, and help maintain the required illusion until the spirit had made a sufficient adjustment to deal realistically with its new situation.

Hyslop identified two bodies of information. One suggested that the future life would have to involve a world with the main features of the present one, except that they would not be accessible to the physical senses. Others hold that the world beyond death is structured of energies entirely mental. "They are not," said Hyslop, "necessarily contradictory." They are, in fact, already combined in the life of the present world; we all have lives of external perception, as well as lives of internal consciousness, reflection, imagination, and meditation. There is no reason, the great researcher maintained, why some such combination might not prevail in the universe beyond death, though perhaps with a somewhat different "mix."

V

The Revelations of Frederic Myers

WITHOUT, for the moment, raising questions of priorities or precedents between mental and physical things, let us now consider how large a part of our normal workaday lives is taken up with structures which are made of nothing but pure thought. For the sake of illustration, I should like to begin with some quite commonplace examples.

In our present world, mental and physical structures are inextricably mixed. I feel a desire for some companionship (mental). I pick up the telephone (physical) and make arrangements (mental) to meet a friend at a specific place and time (physical). Our voice boxes create vibrations in the air (physical), which are received as words (mental), which are immediately translated into companionship (mental).

Children in most of the United States are required by law to spend twelve years in school. A large part of their time there is expected to be spent in purely mental activity—taking in organized thought impressions, processing them with their own mental activity, and demonstrating to the satisfaction of their teachers a resulting thought structure of their own. A very large part of the business world is thought. An inventive mind gets an "idea" (mental) for a product, a book, a building, a new customer (physical). His idea is given physical expression in drawings and memoranda which transfer it to the minds (mental) of others, who now translate it into *physical* "reality."

The extent to which thought structures dominate our present world of physical existence is much greater than is generally realized. Every article of clothing we put on, every appliance, utensil, piece of furniture, every vehicle we use, every structure we dwell in or enter, every coin we give or receive, every action we take, every movement in which we participate all owe their existence to an original act of pure thought. Even nature partakes of this mental quality. The song of the thrush, the shape of the flower, when traced to their origins, are found to originate in mysterious structured forces which are in their essential nature mental.

When analyzed, the physical "realities" which have become so dear to our senses and so seemingly necessary to our physical activities turn out to be just as mysterious as, and resulting from, the mental world. Physicists tell us that this physical world is made up of a combination of electromagnetic and inertia-gravitational forces. We can give names to the forces and observe some of their effects, but no one can say what they really are.

So with the world of thought—the mental world. Each of us, in the humdrum routines of daily existence, spends a good deal of his time in this world. Poets and musicians, who spend nearly all their time in it, speak with assurance of esthetic structures which are as real and as solid to them as structures of steel and stone are to the building contractor (whose edifice began with an immaterial thought in the mind of an architect) . In every area of our lives, no matter what our age or occupation, we encounter the inescapable prior reality of thought forms.

In what native environment do these thought forms live? Through what medium are they transferred? Beyond the clearly established fact that mental energy operates according to laws that are independent of the laws governing physical phenomena, science can say very little in answer to these questions. A century of experimentation in hypnosis, telepathy, and telekinesis has proved that thought energy can be directly transmitted at a distance and that it easily penetrates barriers which stop all other forms of energy. Recently, Soviet researchers have demonstrated that thought energy can impart visible motion to physical objects. The American polygraph expert Cleve Backster has shown that human thought directed at plant cells penetrate the electromagnetic shielding, as well as thick barriers of lead and concrete. The psychically gifted Ted Serios has shown U.S. researchers that it can impress a picture on film.

We do not have to invoke anything occult, then, to establish the basis for our next step in the comprehension of the life beyond death. The two necessary precepts have a vast experimental foundation: First, structures of pure thought are of primary importance in human life. Second, such structures may exist in human society and in nature independently of any physical phenomena. These two statements, here asserted as axioms, form the bridge between the world of our gross physical senses and the world of the life beyond, which is largely, if not entirely, a mental world.

The case of Frederic Myers is of special interest to those of our own time who believe there is a distinct possibility of a life after death and would like to know more about its conditions and quality. This is not only because Myers was an original, energetic, resourceful, dedicated, and highly intelligent psychical researcher for thirty years before his "death" and for thirty years after it. Ancient and modern history, as well as contemporary journalism, offers unnumbered examples of people who had an active curiosity about the life beyond death while in the physical realm and who found means to report back after emerging into the life beyond bone, flesh, and tissue. But most of these people have talked in some idiom other than the language of credence of our time. They may talk in the imagery of poetry, or of religion, or of mythology, or of art, or of common speech. In our time, none of these are believed. When listened to at all, they are not taken seriously or regarded as fact. The language of credence of our day is the idiom of physical or psychological science.

This is Myers' special strength. A highly educated man and professor at Cambridge, one of the world's leading universities, he was a classical scholar best known for his perceptive essays on the Roman poets before he found his life's work in psychical research. He was thoroughly familiar with the physical and theoretical science that led to Einstein's discoveries and with the basic insights of modern psychology up to and including Freud.

Myers began his researches in a deeply skeptical mood. He and his associates were the most ruthless iconoclasts and exposers of fraud ever known. Their standards of evidence were so rigid that some bitterly called his research group, a "society for the suppression of evidence." It was only the relentless pressure of the steadily accumulating evidence that finally persuaded Myers that the survival of human personality beyond death was a fact. After that, he saw the main problem not as establishing truth—this had been done—but of communicating that truth in terms a mass mind sunk deep in the dogma of physical science could comprehend.

No one was more profoundly familiar with the depth and subtleties of the scientific problems of survival research than was Myers. No one was more intimately acquainted with the legitimate basis for scientific skepticism than he was. Immersed as we are in the dogma of physical science from kindergarten, we need to hear new ideas in our familiar language in order to believe them. It is this, rather than its uniqueness, that gives Myers' testimony its special value. He "talks our language."

At the time of Myers' death in 1901, the two great obstacles already mentioned still stood in the way of a general acceptance of the fact of survival. One was the telepathy-of-the-living hypothesis. Once telepathy had been established as a real and continuous phenomenon, there was a rush to explain all communications claiming to originate in the world beyond death as conscious or unconscious fabrications of the medium, who was presumed to gather his information by searching the contents of living human minds. Myers acknowledged this as a legitimate, if improbable, objection. He sought constantly to devise demonstrations which would conclusively rule out every possibility of origin in physical protoplasm. After his "death" he neatly solved the problem in the famous cross correspondences.

The second major difficulty was the lack of any generally accepted theoretical basis on which a materialistically oriented scientist might build a conceptual structure of a continuing and expanding life. This he solved by demonstrating thought energy and thought forms, using language already familiar to psychologists.

It is not necessary to understand scientific terminology in order to understand Myers. We have all heard the expression "He is lost in thought." Myers might ask, "Lost to what?" To be sure, he is lost to the "realities" of the workaday world. But science has shown us that these realities are illusory. The table that looks so solid, the human body that appears so substantial are, science has shown us, mostly empty space. The great relative distances between the small nucleus and the circling electrons of the atom show that all appearance of solidity is illusion in space. The man lost in thought is in a mental world where no such illusions exist. Myers—and a great many other people—would insist that the true case is exactly the opposite. People who never entered the mental realm, these would say, are the truly lost—they are sleepwalking robots. The man "lost" in thought is actually approaching the true and the only reality, since ultimate reality is mental in nature.

The cross correspondences were messages received over Myers' signature by automatic writers in trance after Myers' death. The messages came in fragments so that no one communication through any one medium made any sense. When these fragments were pieced together according to instructions (a matter made easy by the clearinghouse system in use at the time), they made a perfectly clear, consecutive, and sensible communication. Mediums were selected who did not know one another and who had little or no knowledge of the obscure classical sources Myers habitually used, in addition to his signature, to identify himself. The general character, continuity, and governing personality of these messages did not change for a quarter century, though several sets of mediums were used. The early mediums dropped out by death, pressure of circumstance, or other causes and were replaced by new mediums, some of whom had not known of the cross correspondences, all having no understanding of classical literature.

We may take up Myers' elucidation of the circumstances of the life beyond death at a sitting with Mrs. Leonard during which Sir Oliver Lodge had been in communication with his son Raymond. Lodge had not known Myers in earth life. The great physicist's interest in psychical research began early in this century, shortly after Myers' death. The acquaintance of the two men was entirely "inter-world."

Lodge told his son about a statement given by Myers through another medium to the effect that the plane of existence Raymond was now in was what we would call illusion. Lodge wanted to know what Raymond thought of this statement. Raymond explained that Myers, whom he had come to know well enough to address familiarly as "Uncle Fred," was with them at that very moment and that together they would try to clear up the matter. (Difficulties of terminology frequently turn up in such communications; it seems to be rather like explaining what snow and ice are like to a tropical native who has never experienced either.) Raymond explained that there were many parallels between the plane on which he and Myers were living and the plane on which his father was living. On both planes, Raymond said, many of the things we need are created for us by the divine imagination and many more—houses, clothes, jewels, and so on —are created out of our own imaginations. In both cases the necessities are created out of available materials. And in both cases the structures are temporary, meant for use only until the individual had been readied to progress to the next higher plane of life. In earth-side living our objects were made out of what we choose to call matter. In Raymond's sphere the necessities were made out of much finer material created by the power of mind.

"You live in a world of illusions," said Raymond, "—illusions necessary to enable you to do your work. We live in an extension of the illusory world in which you live. The outer rim of it. We are more in touch with the world of reality than you are. Spirit and mind belong to the world of reality. Everything else, that is, external things, are in a sense necessary for a time, but superfluous and only temporary as far as the world of reality goes. Spirit and mind belong to that world and are indestructible."

The bulk of Myers' discourse on the afterworld came through an Irish girl, Geraldine Cummins of Cork. Myers did not begin his serious discussion of after-death living until he had been in his new surroundings for more than twenty years and had completed a great deal of cross correspondence and other work designed to demonstrate the fact of survival. Miss Cummins was not a professional medium. Daughter of a professor, she had no education in science, psychology, or philosophy, but was interested in the theater and had written two plays which had been produced at the Abbey Theater. Her habit when about to write automatically was to sit down, cover her eyes with her left hand, and concentrate on the thought of stillness. This induced a "kind of half-sleep or dream-state." When the automatic writing began, it was "as if an endless telegram were being tapped out" through her arm by a stranger she was willing to help. Her right hand rested on a large pad of paper and someone stood by to remove the pages as they were filled and replace her hand for each new sheet. The writing was very rapid. Normally, Miss Cummins said she would need seven or eight hours to write a short article of perhaps 800 words. In automatic writing she turned out as much as 2,000 words in a little more than an hour. The material seemed to have been organized in advance, for rapid presentation, complete with chapter headings— but without punctuation, paragraphing or spaces between the words, which all ran together continuously. Myers outlined the structure and conditions of life beyond death in considerable detail, transmitting in all, between the years 1924 and 1931, enough to fill an average-size book.

If we are to grasp the full import of Myers' message, it would be well to review at this point the concept which, though never specifically stated by him, permeates the whole of his communication—evolution-of-consciousness or post-Darwinian evolutionary theory. According to this hypothesis, as developed during the twentieth century by Bergson, Bucke, Julian Huxley, Teilhard, Jung, Meda-

war, and others, the main thrust of evolution is to develop an increasing capacity for breadth and depth of
awareness, with the multiplicity of physical forms a mere
by-product of this central evolutionary drive.

Earthworms, clams, and barnacles, possessing "simple
consciousness" live in a dim dream, living out their lives
in a few cubic feet of earth space, dimly aware of light,
dark, heat, cold, hunger, and a need to reproduce. On the
reptile, bird, and animal scale, consciousness ascends
through a hierarchy of awarenesses of increasing range.
In the human world, the outstanding feature of progression from infancy to adulthood is an extension of the
range of things the individual can be aware of. When
adulthood is achieved, there still remain vast differences
in capacities for—"levels of"—awareness. The consciousness of woman A may be limited to husband, house, children, and shopping centers, while the mind of woman B
may encompass all these things and also an appreciation
of music, an interest in books, participation in local politics.

The awareness levels of both women may change.
Woman A may suddenly develop an interest in religion
which may open her eyes to the predicament of the entire
human species and set her off on a serious study of international affairs. Woman B may, in addition to her present interests, develop an intense concern for social justice
and thus increase her understanding of social machinery.
Both women will have, on this present earth plane, to use
a phrase frequently employed by Myers, "progressed to a
higher level of consciousness." Similarly, the man ob-
sessed with stock market, family, and fishing may develop
an interest in art and languages and thus expand his level
of consciousness without ever leaving the earth plane.

The Myers communications assert that the evolution-ary thrust toward ever-expanding awareness is cosmic and eternal and hence does not stop at death. The main thrust of creation is not physical forms but mental ones, easily capable of casting off one physical form to take on another or existing in abundant, energetic life with no physical form at all. The wise human being on earth, if he has kept himself mentally alert, progresses toward wis-dom through ever-widening and ever-deepening under-standing of physical, mental, and spiritual principles.

So, Myers says, do we progress in the life beyond death. In the life on earth, as a by-product of our growing con-sciousness, we take on and discard numerous bodies—those of infants, preadolescents, adolescents, young adults, mature adults, and several adult-body replace-ments. In the life beyond death, not only does the evolutionary thrust toward widening awareness continue, but it is also housed in a sequence of bodies. These life-beyond bodies, however, are made of lighter, finer, more highly energized materials, with an increasing content of mental-spiritual energy as the sequence progresses. The Creator Himself is conceived as pure creative thought-energies source—"The Great Imagination."

Myers, after twenty years of "other-side" experience and observation, conceived the after-death life experi-ence as divided into seven major stages, each with its entry phase, period of development, and period of preparation for the next higher stage. Stage One is, of course, the earth plane. Stage Two is the condition of the individual immediately after death. Myers refers to it variously as "The Life Immediately After Death," "The Intermediate Plane," and "Hades." This stage is brief and is followed by entry into a more stable world Myers calls "The Plane of Illusion" or "The Immediate World After Death."

There follows Stage Four, an indescribably lovely existence called "The Plane of Color" or "The World of Eidos." Highly qualified souls may now progress to the "The Plane of Flame" or "The World of Helios," which is Stage Five. The ultimate stages Six and Seven—"The Plane of Light" and "Timelessness"—are of an advanced spiritual nature, so close to the ultimate essence of creativity that no experience vocabulary has yet been evolved to describe them, and hence they are difficult to communicate to earth-level beings. The situation is roughly analogous to, but far more difficult than, that of the earth-side doctor trying to explain the action of the endocrine glands to a kindergarten child whose endocrine glands he is treating.

Myers illustrates this progression with case histories. There should be one further preliminary word before continuing Myers' discourse: on reincarnation. At the time when Myers was writing, both on the earth plane and, through mediums, from the afterlife, the reincarnation theory was not given wide credence among Western psychologists, parapsychologists, and psychical researchers. Since then, and particularly in the light of the very recent investigations of the University of Virginia professor of psychology Ian Stevenson, the likelihood of reincarnation is being taken much more seriously. In this respect, as well as in evolution-of-consciousness theory, Myers proved himself well ahead of his time.

As Myers' first case history, we may consider the instance of "Walter." Walter was one of the four sons of a middle-class family able to live comfortably on the income produced by the father's unimaginative and repetitious occupation. It was a "family-centered" family, dominated by a mother who found adequate life fulfillment in directing the affairs of her children, of whom she was very proud. The family was smug, proud, and aloof, considering themselves somewhat above the general run of humanity and entering hardly at all into human affairs outside the family circle.

Walter was a particular favorite of both his parents. He finally married, but the marriage had a brief life. Walter, so long accustomed to the unqualified praise heaped upon him by his mother, could not adjust to the presence of a woman who assessed him more realistically. There were bitter quarrels and finally a divorce. Walter returned to home and mother, and devoted his surplus energies to making money. An adroit stock manipulator, he was very successful and amassed a great deal of money. After the death of his mother and father, he moved to an expensive and well-appointed city club and there lived out the rest of his earth days enjoying the adulation the earth plane heaps upon the man who has a lot of money. Walter eventually died and entered Stage Two, the "Intermediate Plane" or "Hades."

When a baby emerges from the fetus level of consciousness to earth awareness, he does a good deal of sleeping, dreaming, and resting, while people more accustomed to the earth plane attend to his needs, of which he is but dimly aware. So it is, says Myers, with the entry into Stage Two. In the tradition of folklore, people anticipating immediate death are said to have memories of their entire past lives flash before them. If this is true, it would seem to be a preview of Myers' Intermediate Plane or Hades. During this interval Walter was, when not sleeping, in a resting state of drowsy reverie in which memory pictures of his past life floated through his mind. Apparently it is this state which is referred to in the ancient tradition of "hell." Whether or not it is "hellish," of course, depends upon the memory content of the particular psyche. If this contains sinister episodes and terrifying experiences, these will drift by the dreamer's vision along with the more joyful happenings. Myers designates this interval "The Journey Down the Long Gallery."

During Walter's sleepy journey down this memory path, he rediscovered his old affection for his mother and the pleasant, admiring protective glow of affection with which she had surrounded him. As he became stronger, and his imaginative force more potent, he found himself able to re-create an idealized version of the old home, the old hometown and—in cooperation with the still willing and still possessive psyche of his mother—live happily among circumstances he considered ideal.

In Stage Three—"The Plane of Illusion" or "The Immediate World After Death"—materials are so pliable that they may be shaped by direct action of the imagination. They do not, as in the case of the recalcitrant materials of the earth plane, have to pass through the hands of draftsmen, blueprinter, and workman. Walter now had no problems except an excess of time on his hands. Since he had always loved the old game of buying and selling stocks, he looked around for others who might like to play the game with him—and, of course, found them. As on earth, he was very successful and again made a great deal of money. Here, however, the gathering of money did not bring the same admiration and power it had on earth. Since any need could be gratified by the direct action of the imagination, there was no need of money, and few people cared much about it. This produced in Walter a feeling of disappointed restlessness. The feeling was intensified as he began to see that his mother's love for him was childish and possessive. She was a child mother playing with her baby, a little girl playing with her doll.

Nor was his father's admiration of him the same as it had been. The father was one of those who saw little point in making money in a place where it was not needed. Gradually Walter was brought face to face with the fact that, spiritually, he did not amount to much. Trapped between his father's scorn and his mother's suffocating possessiveness, he was driven to a frustrated rage. He felt he had to get out of there. The question was —to where? He longed more and more for the old days of excitement in the stock market, where he was the center of many admiring eyes. He began to feel "what is called the earth pull, the birth pull." He regressed to Stage Two, where he again reviewed his past experience. There he made his decision to return to Stage One, the earth plane. He would be born again as a human baby as soon as appropriate parents could be found and would try again to see what he could learn from further experiences of earth life.

Walter had a brother named Martin who had been killed in a war many years before Walter's death. There had also been a sister, Mary, who had died young. Mary and Martin had wider horizons than their brother Walter or their parents. Both had, through earth-life adventures that had taken them far outside the narrow preoccupations of the family circle, awakened in themselves the possibilities of a loving concern for all humanity.

They, too, after a period in the Stage Two dream rest, had returned to the imaginatively created old-hometown surroundings and enjoyed a family reunion. But their stay at this level of consciousness was brief. They quickly saw the limitations of housekeeping and stock trading, no matter how pleasantly these occupations might be idealized. They longed, not for return to earth life, but for great, awareness-increasing experiences in entirely new dimensions. And so they went on to the "Plane of Color" or "Eidos."

Eventually, all the children gone, even father and mother began to reconsider the hometown situation. The mother, drawn back to earth by her attachment to Walter, would reenter Stage One as an earth baby. There, by living a life of wider awareness and generosity, she would redeem the damage her possessiveness had caused the last time around. The wavering father had no desire to return to earth. At last, with the anonymous help of Martin from Eidos, he was guided along a path that would lead him to strive for the next higher level of consciousness.

Not all experiences on the third plane, Myers says, are as stuffy as those described in the case of this family. The grouping urge, instead of being a family structure, may be a special interest, a religion, a profession, a trade, an art or almost anything that would join people in a joint exercise of their imaginations. Since communication is by direct-image telepathy, there are no language barriers. And since enthusiasms are no respecters of centuries, time is of little account. So it is perfectly possible for a soul to find itself part of a group containing people from other nations and from other centuries.

Though an individual may linger in Stage Three for generations, an eventual decision must be made: The individual either returns to earth or progresses to Stage Four. Before leaving, however, the more enterprising souls may have an opportunity to experience one of the great wonders of this plane of consciousness—a tour through some section of The Great Memory. Just as, on earth, one may go to a film library and see newsreels of important earth events since the invention of the motion-picture camera, so, in Stage Three, one may witness the originals of desire-selected events from the beginning of human experience. Everything that has ever happened has been recorded by the cosmic memory.

"I have journeyed only as far as Eidos, the Fourth Plane," Myers wrote by the hand of Miss Cummins, ". . . so my knowledge is necessarily restricted." Here, as on the earth plane, he sees himself as "an explorer" into the ultimate nature of human life and of the universe and of the relationships between the two. His clear, conscious aim is to penetrate as far as he can into the mystery being successively revealed to him, then, through sensitives, to send back word of newly discovered territories to "the collective mind of man." Gradually he leads us to see a cosmic *process* at work. The traveler who will persevere in the arduous business of increasing the range of his sensitivity and understanding will, stage by stage, find himself growing in perception of ever more extensive ranges of the creative universe.

One receives an impression that it is the aim of the

Creator to "take into the firm," as junior partners, as many as can qualify. As soon as earth experience has been thoroughly comprehended—either through one or more return trips to that plane, or through exchange of experience with other travelers met on the third plane—the candidate may proceed to realms beyond the reach of the earth mind. "If you are a soul now," Myers writes "—an intelligent ethically developed soul—you will desire to go up the ladder of consciousness. In most cases, the longing for a physical earth-existence will have been burned into ashes."

Throughout Myers' long series of discourses he emphasizes that what he is talking about is the actual *experience* of other modes of existence rather than mere theorizing about them. "Here on the Fourth Plane one must leave behind all rigid intellectual structures and dogmas, be they scientific, religious, or philosophical." Myers is so insistent on this point that he subtitles the fourth plane "The Breaking of the Image." On "The Plane of Color," Myers finds himself for the first time having difficulty verbalizing in earth terms what he is experiencing. "A human being cannot imagine a new sound, a new color or feeling entirely outside the range of his previous experience. It is impossible for him to conceive the infinite variety of new sounds, colors and feelings experienced by us on the Fourth Plane."

He can, however, communicate certain of its qualities. The demands of the earth body, the presuppositions of earth forms, the effects of their long imprint and conditioning, while still in memory, are now put far behind. A new and more highly energized intellect and spirit find a much wider freedom to function. This new energy requires a new body to give it expression and so creates one. It bears a faint resemblance to the old earth form, but is far more radiant and beautiful and better suited to its new employment. Myers continues:

> Flowers are there, but in shapes unknown to you, exquisite in color, radiant with light. Such colors and lights, not contained within any earthly octave, are expressed by us in thoughts and not in words. Words for us are obsolete. The soul, in this plane of consciousness, must struggle and labor, know sorrow but not earth sorrow. Know ecstasy but not earth ecstasy. Mind expresses itself more directly: we can hear the thoughts of other souls. Experience on the fourth plane leads the soul to the borders of the superterrestrial region.

In this plane, Myers says, everything is unbelievably more intense, more highly energized. Consciousness is continuous; sleep is no longer necessary. Experiences are "indescribably" more intense. Not only love, truth, and beauty are present here but also hostility, hate, and anger. "A hostile mentality may, with a powerful projection of thought, blast and wither some part of your body of light and color. You have to learn how to send out protecting rays. If on earth some other man or woman was your enemy and you hated one another the old emotional memory will awaken when you meet. Love and hate draw you inevitably together in the pattern of your particular designs."

The main work on this plane is toward further understanding of how mind controls energy and life-force, from which all outward appearances emerge. Here one is free from the heavy mechanical restrictions of earth. "I have but to concentrate my thought for what you might call a moment," Myers says, "and I can build up a likeness of myself, send that likeness speeding across our vast world to a friend, to one, that is, in tune with me. Instantly I appear before that friend, though I am remote from him. My likeness holds speech—in thought, remember, not words—with this friend. Yet, all the time, I control it from an enormous distance; and as soon as the interview is concluded I withdraw the life of my thought from that image of myself, and it vanishes."

Since Myers had not progressed beyond the fourth plane at the time of his communication, his accounts of the higher levels of consciousness beyond this are less detailed and more speculative. He seems to have picked up enough hearsay, however, to outline with some confidence the general nature of the further advance.

A death experience and a rebirth are required, he says, as a transition from each stage to the next higher. It is assumed that on the fourth plane the intense experience of "profound despair and inconceivable bliss" has burned away the last vestiges of the cumbersome pettiness and animosities of earth, finally and completely freed the soul from domination by that planet. The spirit is now qualified to experience cosmic ranges beyond earth's confines. In the fifth plane one acquires a body of flame, enabling him to tour the stellar universe without being harmed by its temperatures and turbulence and to return with a fuller experience of these cosmic reaches. The sixth plane is "The Plane of Light." Individuals on this plane are matured spirits, having lived through, with conscious comprehension, all the aspects of the created universe.

Myers calls this "The Plane of White Light" and subtitles it "Pure Reason." Souls on this plane are described as follows:

> They bear with them the wisdom of form, the incalculable secret wisdom, gathered only through limitation, harvested from numberless years, garnered from lives passed in myriad forms. . . . They are capable of living now without form, of existing as white light in the pure thought of their creator. They have joined the immortals . . . fulfilled the final purpose of the evolution of consciousness.

The seventh and final stage—in which the soul enters full partnership with God—is beyond Myers' verbal reach. It "baffles description; it is heart-breaking even to attempt to write of it."

Myers knew that the levels of consciousness in the upper ranges were beyond the insight of the average earth dweller except for intuitive flashes. He gives us such detail about worlds beyond our reach, I believe, simply to assure us that there *are* such worlds. They are attainable to us and to our loved ones whenever the desire to attain them is strong enough. He wanted to remove from the human mind once and for all any fear of death with the assurance that there is no death, only alterations in mode of consciousness.

As a practicing, professional trance medium, I have dealt mainly in those regions designated by Myers as the second and third planes. Only occasionally have the spiritual transactions in which my transmission facilities been utilized tapped the very high regions of spiritual development. These cases I have discussed in other writings. Here I am concerned with those aspects of the life beyond death which assert themselves most frequently and most acceptably to the comprehension of the average earth mind—that is, the second and third planes. Myers gives such abundant insight here that I believe it will be well worth our while to attend to what he has to say about the life-death transactions most familiar to earth-side experience.

Though flashes of spirit light may occasionally and briefly illuminate the darkness of the average earth mind, the afterlife business most often brought to its attention concerns only the immediate death transition and the third stage. Very large numbers of average souls remain comfortably in this third stage for very long periods—sometimes many centuries—imagining it to be the ultimate heaven and making no effort to progress further.

When we recall that Myers was writing through Miss Cummins in the early 1930's, we are surprised at the contemporary sound of some of the things he has to say. Population explosion, environmental pollution, military-industrial conspiracies to make war, domination of human spirit by mechanical and political machines, over-attachment to earth possessions—all themes prominent in the more thoughtful press of our time—were subjects of solemn warnings by Myers, writing through Miss Cummins, a generation ago.

It is commonly (and mistakenly) believed that people mysteriously acquire the ability to foretell the future after they have passed into the afterlife. Though they cannot predict events, they can discern trends; this is something a little different. "No man is permitted to know in full the secret of the coming time," Myers wrote. "But we souls who dwell in . . . Eidos dimly see the trend of man's thought and therefore, presage his endeavor in the coming time." His clear observation of these trends evoked his profound concern: "I beg of the men and women of the day to consider the human being apart from machines, to consider life apart from gold. Within the restless jangle of those monstrous cogs and wheels which now turn ceaselessly and bear your so-called civilization upon them, there is little leisure or quiet for the calmness or philosophic meditation out of which knowledge is born. What somber destiny may not awake the children of the morrow if they, too, are caught in the grip of that creature without a soul, the machine— that last and final embodiment of the god of materialism."

Myers points to the dangers of runaway nationalistic feelings which splinter mankind into mutually hating and fearing national groups. This delays the awareness that mankind is one, and its problems cannot be solved until they are solved jointly. "The nations may plunge down the hill into war, or produce and propagate misery by an increase in its millions of human beings." As for environment: "Neither beauty nor health can survive and flourish when nation destroys nation and machine destroys machine." Machine thinking endangers man's spiritual evolution: "A mechanism without a soul should be the servant, not the master, of the thinking human being. The world of today should envisage the ideal of quality, not quantity."

People have often asked me about the status in the afterlife of suicides. Myers' position on suicide is less moralistic than practical. The extreme negative, depressed mental state of the suicide at the time of his self-destructive act carries over into the afterlife, placing him at a great disadvantage in making his adjustment. Many times, upon awakening, he does not realize that he has passed over. He may go into an extreme panic upon discovering that he can no longer control his physical body. Upon reaching full realization that he has in fact killed himself, he may—as in the case of the son of the late Bishop James Pike, in which I was able to be of some help—deeply regret his act.

In the Pike case, the young man committed suicide while undergoing a destructive LSD experience. On discovering his plight, he was desperate. He produced every kind of poltergeist effect within his power—smashing things, disarranging clothing, moving objects, bending and distributing safety pins, moving books that would call attention to his memory—all to attract help in his plight. The bishop finally caught the hint and sought the assistance of mediums, including myself. The boy's whole desperate story then came through, and forces were set going to help him.

"The mood that drives the suicide to self-slaughter," Myers wrote through Miss Cummins, "will envelop him like a cloud from which we may not for a long time be able to give him release. His emotional thoughts, his whole attitude of mind sets up a barrier which can only be broken down by his own strenuous efforts, by a brave control of himself, and above all by the call sent out with all the strength of his soul to higher beings to bestow succour, to grant release."

"Sudden death," mentioned in the famous litany and

commonplace in our time of war and highway accident, is another theme that has produced many questions. Again Myers takes the practical view. The disadvantage of a sudden death, he says, lies mainly in the circumstance that the psyche has no time to adjust. A person suddenly killed in his prime may linger among earth scenes for some time before the realization of his new situation reaches him. In this state of mind he is slow to understand the need for the help of other discarnate beings in making his adjustment and hence is slow to utilize this help. However, there have been many cases in my own experience as a medium in which death which came suddenly has seemingly been handled without great deviation from the normal, comfortable transition. The normal transition, Myers says, is a simple and peaceful going into a pleasant, sometimes even blissful, totally restful sleep. During this period the astral body—that radiant "double" which accompanies our physical body from the fetal stage and which is clearly visible to psychics gifted with the ability to see auras—detaches itself.

This body, though sleeping, is as alive as ever, though now existing exclusively in the consciousness wavelengths allotted to astral bodies. As the rest continues, there may be dreams involving memories of earth life. Upon awakening the soul is usually met and welcomed by friends, vocational associates, and relatives who made this transition before him.

Myers did not disapprove the use of drugs to ease and speed the passage of persons suffering an incurable disease, though he thought several days should be allowed for the transition. "Under these conditions the merciful physician is entirely justified in committing what the law still holds to be murder." A great deal more under-standing of disease will come, he says, when doctors begin to see the connection between body and spirit.

What is the effect of brain damage or advanced senility on the afterlife? Here, Myers reminds us that the "double" or astral body, the vehicle of the personality after death, is with us from conception. Everything known to the physical body is also known to the astral body. Brain damage, he says, can only make the individual "unable to *manifest* his intelligence to the visible world of men. He is still intellectually alive . . . after death, the soul finds his fundamental memory center in his astral body. . . . He or she has only withdrawn a little way from you and has no need of your pity."

There has been much speculation about how the body sustains itself without food. Myers explains: "Etheric life is nourished by cosmic rays that splendidly light up our surroundings and—in some manner I do not understand —sustain the life of our bodies." There have been cases of earth dwellers—specifically the famous German mystic Therese Neumann and a saintly old Indian woman known to Yogananda—who were able to utilize these rays for physical nourishment on earth. They sustained themselves without food for many years. Just how this was managed is a secret not understood even by such advanced spirits as Yogananda. It is reported here simply as an empiric fact.

Myers expressed the opinion that other planets carry life resembling ours. He does not believe that the failure of our senses and instrumentation to detect them can be taken as evidence. We perceive, he says, only those wave-lengths which our "sets" are tuned to perceive. In electromagnetic reception, a radio or television tuned to a given station will not register messages from another broadcasting station even though this be nearby and broadcasting a powerful signal. He emphasizes that all worlds occupy the same space. Our inability to perceive anything other than earth phenomena affects in no way the fact that superterrestrial, cosmic, and spiritual activity of incredible intensity is at all times in progress around us.

VI

The Afterworld Appeals to Science:
"Betty" and "Joan"

DURING THE 1950's a discarnate personality who gave her name as Ruth Finley spoke out at one of my sittings in response to a sitter who had been persistently questioning about the nature of the afterworld consciousness. During seven different sittings, Mrs. Finley sent messages with specific answers for the questioning sitter. Then, one day, she presented a carefully prepared statement on the mechanics of trance mediumship.

We must bear in mind, she said, that each individual is an energy complex involving a physical body and a mental-emotional body. The physical body is made of one kind of energy moving at a relatively low rate of vibration. Within its frequency span the various organs—heart, liver, brain—have varying frequencies. Interpenetrating this pattern of physical energies is a distinct mental-emotional body, vibrating at entirely different frequencies and composed of much finer energies, which is generally known as the beta or astral body.

These finer energies remain unaffected by death. When the physical-level vibrations cease, the beta body—soul— separates itself, graduating to its proper milieu in the freer space and more intense energies of the unob- structed universe.

Everything, Mrs. Finley explained, is energy in some form. Our natural world is full of examples of different energy forms existing side by side in the same entity— heat-light in a fireplace, heat-light-electricity in a light bulb, electricity-magnetism-motion-momentum in an electric motor, and so on. In the earth-side electrical par- allels, the prime energy is electricity. In the total uni- verse, the prime energy—and director of all other ener- gies—is consciousness. Though all consciousness units have finer rhythms than can be perceived by our five gross physical senses, there are variations within units. All radio waves have a different frequency from all heat waves, but individual broadcasting stations can be iden- tified within the radio frequencies. Similarly, individual beta bodies have characteristic vibrations, and this fact is of utmost importance in understanding the mental me- chanics of mediumship.

In normal earth-side living, said Mrs. Finley (through my vocal cords, of course, while I was in trance) , there is constant interplay between the mental-emotional and the physical-cellular energies. Therefore, if the medium's mental-emotional body wishes to detach itself for any length of time, then some other mental-emotional unit, with an energy pattern of about the same frequency, must cooperate with the medium's body energy to main- tain its normal state. Thus, for the time being, the discarnate personality becomes a physically living individual in that he inhabits—although not completely—a living human body. Thus, said Ruth Finley, it is Ford who is "dead" while his physical body is occupied by Fletcher. However, the exchange could not be permanent even if Ford were willing.

Although Ruth Finley's communication contained some novelties of analogy and some fresh information, it did not add significantly to what had already been known about the nature of communication in trance. What impressed me most about these communications, when I heard of them, was not so much what was said as who was saying it.

The twentieth century, like every other century, has produced innumerable examples of persons who have "returned" to give us, through mediums, information about the nature and quality of the life beyond death. However, these communications are notoriously uneven in quality. We have very few records as self-consistent, as cogently reasoned, as sensitively described, and as charged with conviction—and transmitted over so long a span of time—as those of Frederic Myers.

This same Ruth Finley was involved in one of the few carefully recorded sets of communications that compare favorably in all respects with the Myers sequence. This sequence is, in fact, a sort of complement to Myers. Where Myers sketched the whole range of consciousness from birth to eternity, the American sequence concentrated on the energy mechanics of a single portion of the afterlife spectrum, Myers' "Third Plane." Ruth Finley's cooperation was essential to the completion of this historic psychic achievement.

When living earth-side, Mrs. Finley was, by any standard, an extraordinary woman. Born in Akron, Ohio, Ruth Ebright attended Oberlin College and the University of Akron, then went to Cleveland to get a job on a newspaper. There she met Emmet Finley, an attorney turned newspaperman, whom she married. She was continuously active in journalism and in public life. Starting as editor of the women's page of the Cleveland *Press,* she became fiction editor of the Scripps-Howard chain, then managing editor of the Washington *Herald,* then women's editor of a newspaper syndicate. Turning to magazine work, she was associate editor of *McClure's Magazine,* then editor of a women's political review. She was a member of the steering committee of the National Federation of Business and Professional Women's Clubs and a trustee of her local public library. She wrote two books in the field of Americana and innumerable newspaper and magazine pieces. Besides all this, she was, anonymously, the author of *Our Unseen Guest,* one of the most widely read books on psychic phenomena of the 1920's. Mrs. Finley, the "Joan" of the "Darby and Joan" team described later, was one of the most gifted trance mediums of the twentieth century, yet she kept her gift so well hidden that even her best friends didn't know she had it! The reason for her anonymity is obvious. Nobody knew better than Ruth Finley, the worldly-wise, practical newspaperwoman, that we live in an age of rigid, bigoted materialism. She shared her gift only with those able to appreciate it.

Among these were Stewart Edward White and his wife, Elizabeth "Betty" Grant White, who also had an almost incredible (by materialistic earth-side standards) tale to tell. White was a naturalist, world traveler, and author of books—some forty in all—on outdoor exploration in all parts of the world. He held bachelor's and master's degrees from the University of Michigan and was a graduate of Columbia Law School. When not traveling, he lived with his wife in Burlingame, California. "Before March 17, 1919," White wrote, "I had paid occult matters very little attention. If called upon to express myself, I suppose I would have taken my stand on the side of skepticism. I knew that spiritualism had been 'exposed.' "

Then, on the date mentioned, some friends called, bringing with them a parlor toy that was a current rage —a ouija board. "The occasion was derisive and gay," at first, White reported; then unexpectedly the board took a serious turn. It suddenly became precise, brisk, and businesslike. "Why do you ask foolish questions?" it spelled, effectively sobering the assembly. Then it began a repeated spelling of the name Betty. Mrs. White, who had taken a brief and scornful trial at the board and then retired from it, was convinced that it was a trick on the part of those sitting to lure her back to the table and was reluctant to return.

Finally, she agreed, however, and the moment her fingers touched the board it responded with a new vitality. "Get a pencil," it spelled; "get a pencil," again and again. Mrs. White had heard of automatic writing, and several days later she actually did "get a pencil," sat with it poised on a sheet of paper, and let herself lapse into blank reverie. The pencil began to move, just as the ouija board indicator had moved. She told her husband about it and showed him the automatic writing.

White's interest was now aroused. He became his

wife's assistant, taking away the filled sheets as his wife wrote and replacing them with fresh ones, taking notes and offering encouragement. Betty was completely unaware of what she was writing. The words came very slowly at first. There was no punctuation, paragraphing, or capitalization, and all the words were run together without separation. The speed increased and in a few weeks had become quite rapid. White developed a profound respect for the communicator, whoever or whatever it might be. The writing was never silly, and the writer refused to be drawn into foolishness. A consistent purpose was announced: to prepare Betty's consciousness to receive and communicate important information.

In September, nearly six months after the automatic writing had begun, the "writer" informed the Whites that it would soon cease. Presently, it did. By now White was thoroughly intrigued. He knew that the writing *might* be the work of Betty's own subconscious. He was also aware of the possibility that it might be the work of a discarnate personality. To White, it didn't matter much. By some means not generally understood, Betty was tapping a level of awareness not commonly accessible. The material was worth having for its own sake.

The Whites persevered. While on a business trip, White read a book called *Our Unseen Guest,* which reported an experience with trance mediumship. When he returned home, he and Betty agreed to try this method. Betty easily achieved the trance state. "She slipped into a kind of freed or double consciousness. From it she reported various experiences. Her speech was at first halting and stumbling, her phrases fragmentary, as though she were having great difficulty. Apparently this was due to the necessity for running two consciousnesses at once. The normal, from which she spoke, was subordinate, it seemed; her real awareness being centered in a deeper consciousness, from which she reported back.

"Progress was exasperatingly slow," White reported. Sometimes a few short sentences would require a whole hour. As with the writing, however, patience was rewarded. Eventually Betty became so fluent in reporting from that "deeper consciousness" that White, an experienced shorthand reporter, sometimes found it hard to keep up.

After a year and a half, White had 400 typewritten pages of notes on what his wife had said during her trances. By this time both were thoroughly convinced that they were dealing with clear-cut, purposeful, outside intelligences and were part of an important project these intelligences were carrying out. The Whites called them the "Invisibles." Their purpose was to produce, with Mrs. White, a "primer of the after-world," which would prepare life voyagers for their eventual destination in a "new country." White "wrote up" these transactions and published them in 1937 as *The Betty Book*.

At first the Invisibles curtly rebuffed the Whites' inquiries about the kind of world they lived in: "You are not yet sufficiently educated to understand our world." Despite this scolding, Betty, during the tentative trips of her center of consciousness into this other domain, made some observations of her own and reported back. On one occasion she observed that it is a "much bigger, nicer place." Another time, she reported that she was being treated exactly as we would treat a newborn baby in this sphere.

Meanwhile, her "education" proceeded. The tragedy of the materialistic age was stated as follows: "You have enfeebled the word 'God.' The world has grown ashamed of the spirit. It mortifies it just as the old ascetics used to mortify the body. . . . Welcome and accept all natural human instincts, all the savoring of life, but permeate them with the vitality of the spirit."

Progress meant action: "Mere intellectual recognition of a truth is aloof, unrelated . . . does not manifest itself in action. . . . It is only by your own determination and faith that you can accomplish that first dead lift." The initial step has to come from earth-side; then "we can utilize what you unconsciously possess" and respond.

"I dimly feel people all around me," Betty said on one occasion, "as one feels people about one in a darkened room. . . . The idea of auras is quite real . . . you go near a fire, and that has an aura of heat; with people it extends just a certain radius around." On one of her "journeys into the beyond" Betty became so curious about how people were nourished that she felt an intense desire herself for sustenance. "I want *nourishment!* It is an instinct toward substance of growth. Curious that sort of nourishment; you don't seem to take it in and give it up again. It is like atoms of power. You add it to the sum of your substance. I don't know just how you do it."

At this point one of the Invisibles interposed: "This goes on quite a while, this collecting substance. Some day you'll get yourself assembled and begin to function over here." In response to a question about how we are seen by those on the other side, this response came: "Our lenses cannot see you as you see yourselves without your physical eyes. Our eyes are for the enduring, different kind of body. Our eyes make real to you the intangible qualities which you call spiritual. Only strainingly do we perceive the material."

In the afterworld, as in the world of dreams, one can shift instantly from one locale to another without cumbersome body movements. "Suppose," said one of the Invisibles, "you could see through a telephone—actually be present at the distant places you communicate with. Does not that dimly give you an idea of entering a wider field of consciousness?" Betty commented: "It seems to be a direct, unobstructed sort of force that carries intelligence from one to another."

Some advice on prayer was offered: "Prayer is an assembling and offering up of your best self for union with the overstrength. . . . Weak prayer does not fulfill its part because it just calls down, instead of rising to meet. . . . It amounts to little *unless* something arises within you to enlarge your capacity to receive it and blend with it. . . . Prayer is the projection of your spiritual being, the conscious assembling of your highest self. In offering up the spirit, you lay bare your own soul, face the sum total of yourself. It pierces all your coverings and trappings as an x-ray pierces the body. There is a terrible reality to it. You must plumb the depths before you are permitted to go on to the heights. There is no discouragement with this facing of one's naked soul. That is the big feeling prayer gives you. It is the workshop of the soul." Betty found prayer reinvigorating: "It's a beautiful form, a grand rhythm. . . . I sweep the whole beauty of a physical world right into my heart, everything, . . . the desert bloom, the frost crystals, the world of the magnifying glass, the stars—all the physical universe—the manifestations of overpowering love and intelligence—I gather them all in my own great rush of worship. It's an offering, a concentration of my life's experience returning to its source. Once spent, I lie still. Quietly, life recharged filters back to me, recharged with vitality, strength and eagerness to take my part."

In regard to levels of consciousness, the Invisibles confirmed Myers, though they declined extensive detail. "You all live together on earth at different levels of consciousness. Certain prerogatives pertain to each level. Yours is the level of dawning perception. It is like going upstairs. Each step must be lived out to the full before we can go on to the next."

A great deal of the three-cornered conversation involving Betty, as medium, the Invisibles, and White was concerned with the principle of service. As one becomes more aware of spiritual principles, one is more and more concerned about the terrible disasters caused by a lack of them. This tends to move one with a spirit of service, taking the form of a desire to share the spiritual insights that would restore harmony. This entails changing people's minds, immediately arousing opposition. Opposition begets opposition, so that one is tempted to be drawn into the same hostility, the same competitive anger which originally caused the loss of spiritual insight and brought upon the world its repetitive disasters. The problem, then, is one of meeting opposition without oneself being drawn into the whirlwind of destructive emotions that opposing forces so often generate.

The Invisibles addressed themselves to this problem with a will, regarding its solution as one of the central building blocks of their teachings. "You cannot

withdraw from the fray; that would be failure. You cannot remain indifferent; that would be cruelty, which is a
spiritual defeat. Though it would be only human, you
cannot be drawn into the vortex of angry emotion; that
only spreads the conflagration."

Then what *can* one do? The advice of the Invisibles
was to place first the principle of maintaining one's own
spiritual poise by focusing one's being on the expanded
consciousness and more fulsome universe which had
come to one. "You cannot pull a friend out of quicksand
unless you have a firm footing yourself." With one's spiritual poise intact, with one's consciousness operating at
its more elevated level, one can then strive, by purely
spiritual projections, to awaken in one's opponent the
same center of spiritual potential which so recently was
awakened in oneself. Thus, said the Invisibles, can one
weather the emotional storms of confrontation and controversy.

Thus was Betty's desire to know more about the life
beyond death diverted by a command to become more
effective, spiritually, in her immediate earth life! The Invisibles did not entirely neglect her curiosity, however.
After driving home their main point—"Fight to win *people*, not victories"—they responded to Betty's desire in a
surprising way.

Here again we encounter the same Ruth Finley who
was later to figure so prominently in the unfolding saga
of Stewart and Betty White and, still later, in my own
mediumship. It happened that, in 1922, eight unusual
persons from various parts of the country were in New
York City for the entire month of January. There were a
newspaperman and his wife, Mr. and Mrs. Gaines. Mrs.

Gaines had demonstrated psychic ability in half trance. There was a business couple; the wife was Margaret Cameron, whose book *The Seven Purposes,* based on her automatic writing, was a best seller at the time. There were the Finleys, whose psychic adventures as "Darby and Joan" had been anonymously reported in the book *Our Unseen Guest* two years previously. And there were the Whites, Stewart and Betty. These eight, all known to each other by reputation, arranged to get together for a series of eleven séances. The results were a sequence of phenomena which none of them had ever produced before and which surprised them all.

The phenomena which now developed were of the "physical" category. This was surprising, since all the psychics in the group were, like myself, of the "mental" sort. At the first séance of this series, the "controls" took over and, speaking through the mediums Betty and Joan (Mrs. Finley) announced that these sittings would be dominated by one clear-cut intent: "To demonstrate the beta body."

If this ethereal body, hitherto visible only to the psychically sensitive, could actually be made visible to the ordinary vision of normal men and women, it would be of tremendous interest to psychical research. It would be a definite, indisputable bridge between "here" and "over there." Such demonstrations had been made, of course, since ancient times. But twentieth-century skepticism writes off everything it has not seen and felt and measured for itself. Further, it discounts as fraudulent or inaccurately reported all reports that do not tally with its materialistic dogma. Here was a nearly ideal research situation. The participants were all well established in the socioeconomic system through achievements quite apart from psychic demonstrations. All had, in fact, begun as skeptics and been at pains to conceal their psychic abilities from general knowledge. Nothing was to be gained by fraud or by distorted reporting.

In sketching in the presuppositions of physical phenomena, I speak with no more authority than any other psychical researcher. Though I have frequently been witness to such events, I do not myself produce them. Here is the traditional and often demonstrated explanation: While living the earth-side existence, the physical body is at all times coincident with a beta body. Though primarily mental, emotional, and spiritual, this beta body retains certain physical aspects during its (following Myers) second and third stages. Unlike the physical body, which is synthetic (an ear or finger can be cut off and the body still live), the beta body is atomic—all of one piece. In earth life as in the second and third stages, this beta body is the residence of the soul—the basic sense of self, the "this is the real me." Under certain special circumstances, the beta body may leave the physical body. This event is the basis for "out-of-body" experiences, bilocation (an individual being clearly seen when his physical body is known to be at a distant point, as in the case of the late Italian monk, Father Pio), and similar events.

The beta body, being the seat of the soul, may command various resources of the physical body when it chooses to. This appears in psychical research as references to "drawing strength," "building up the force," "directing the energy," "ectoplasm," and so on. It is a commonplace of psychical research that mental-spiritual energy takes precedence over and commands physical substance whenever it is sufficiently strong. This has many earth-side parallels and really should surprise no one. Nothing can happen physically until it has first happened mentally; the directing mental act always comes first. Before the bridge can be built, the house erected, or the product manufactured, there must first be the imagined mental structure.

Similarly, physical materials can be reworked at the will of the mind. The cracked bronze bell of yesterday may be melted down to reappear as a bronze statue or as a sound new bell. Recorded physical phenomena suggest that this disintegration and reassembling of substance can be accomplished directly, without the services of intermediary artisans, if the resources are of the necessary kind and power. This has often been demonstrated in the phenomenon called apport, in which objects known to be at a distance are disintegrated, transported, and reassembled in their original condition and made to appear at the scene of the séance.

The White-Gaines-Finley-Cameron sittings were conducted entirely under direction from the "other side." The experimenters in command were entities known as the Doctor, Stephen, Anne (also known as Lady Anne, a Scotswoman who passed over in the seventeenth century and was treated with deference by her discarnate associates), and Joe, the "deceased" son of the Gaineses. The announced intention of the series was accomplished to the satisfaction of all, and other phenomena which had not been scheduled were demonstrated. The beta body of Ruth Finley separated from her physical body and stood for all to see in broad daylight, as well as in a lavender light when evening came, as a luminescent outline. The experimenters said that the beta body was magnetically active and that its presence caused a temperature drop. They directed that instruments be brought to prove these assertions. This was done; the statements proved correct.

In the extensive literature of out-of-body experience, there are frequent references to a "silver cord" connecting the physical and beta bodies. When, in earth life, the beta separates from the physical body, the two bodies remain attached by the silver cord, which is so elastic that the beta may range the entire universe without being severed. On the death of the physical body, the silver cord is released, and the beta body continues, as vehicle of the soul, to the experiences of the second, third, and further planes. In the separation of Joan's beta from her physical body, the silver cord was visible and palpable. This is the same cord made renowned by the Biblical phrase "or ever the silver cord be loosed."

At another sitting, demonstrating the ability of spirit mind to disassemble and reassemble matter, Joan's physical body completely disappeared, on numerous occasions, for thirty seconds or more at a time, to reappear, unchanged, in its original location. Portraits (not the same as beta bodies, but artist's sketches rendered visible in a luminous medium, possibly identical with the substance other researchers have called ectoplasm) of several discarnate personalities were presented. One of them was a sketch of Joan's father; another a portrait of the Gaineses' son. Both were recognizable.

At the end of the experiments, the discarnate researchers summarized their position with reference to that body of dogmatic skepticism which so often masquerades as science. Some progress had been made toward penetrating this wall. Magnetism is now universally acknowledged, and this had been demonstrated. Temperature change is something now universally measurable, and this had been demonstrated. However, the operators were not yet ready for a full confrontation with dogmatic skepticism. "There is no particular value in seeing these masks, or the beta, the stripped soul," Joe Gaines summed up, "except as it has scientific value. There have always been those who could do this, but not from a scientific standpoint. We are not ready for scientists yet."

In 1937 Stewart White published an account of these events in an appendix to *The Betty Book*, which was a narrative of the early years of the mediumship of his wife, Betty.

In April, 1939, Betty died.

Stewart and Betty had been married thirty-five years. Stewart now had reason to recall some of the revelations concerning the life beyond death which were given during the eleven New York sittings. "The *me* as a beta, that *Me* goes on," Joe Gaines had said. "We have form, weight, color, and more senses than you have." Stewart was fully assured of Betty's continued existence. On innumerable occasions—the first one only half an hour after her death—he had vividly sensed her presence beside him, "the cosy, intimate feeling of companionship you get sometimes when you are in the same room, perhaps each reading a book." There were no words, but the experience of companionship was so complete that no words seemed to be necessary. White recalled the advice of discarnates to the effect that communication in the higher realms was direct, spiritual, and wordless. He assumed that their communication would henceforth be on that level and had no clear expectation of further verbal communication.

White flew east on business in September of that year. Emmet and Ruth ("Darby and Joan") Finley now lived in Huntington, Long Island. Of course, there was a séance. It turned out to be the first of many. After six months of silence, Betty now had something to say—something that was important, something she wanted to get across in some detail, something that would take a little time. Stewart, as usual, took careful notes. These were cast into narrative form and published in 1940 under the title *The Unobstructed Universe*.

Betty understood that her first job would be to identify herself beyond any possible question, and she did so without any urging. Through the mediumship of the entranced Joan (Ruth Finley), she began talking to Stewart "quietly, fluently with assured and intimate knowledge of our common experience and living." She poured out "not one, but dozens" of facts drawn from a third of a century of living together that could have been known only to herself and to Stewart—whom she addressed by a nickname used in earth life only by herself, "Stewt."

Once having established her identity, Betty plunged on to the point she was single-mindedly determined to establish as the prime goal of this series of communications: "There is only one universe." In a long series of séances with Joan as medium, she never deviated from this theme except for the purpose of gathering illustrative and supporting material. Thus was created the first fully rounded body of first-person reporting on the life beyond death to be generally circulated since Myers' revelations a quarter of a century earlier. Myers, of course, had been operating from a background of twenty years on the "other side," whereas Betty was speaking from an experience of only a few months. Nevertheless, her testimony has unique value. She had an advantage over Myers in that, possessing mediumistic talent, she had "traveled" in the further realms for twenty years before her passing over. Also, though her experience was presumably limited to the second and third stages, whereas Myers sought to survey the complete range, Betty's explicitness concerning the terrain within her view gives it its own special quality.

"There is only one universe." Whenever I hear this theme song of Betty's, I am reminded of a circumstance reported from one of my own sittings. A newly bereaved widow had come to me in the hope of establishing contact with her deceased husband. The contact was successfully established, she and her husband were in conversation, and she was tearfully relating how desolate she had been "since he went away." The rejoinder came back at once: "But I haven't gone anywhere." This, in essence, is Betty's message. Those of our loved ones who have passed over have not "gone away." They live in the same universe we do. Our main difference is that they have much greater liberties in it. It is in the description of these liberties, and of how it feels to exercise them, that is found the particular strength of Betty's testimony.

Betty employed vivid analogies to illustrate her points: "It is like looking through the moving blades of an electric fan"; "It is like looking at fish in an aquarium"; "It

is the difference between black-and-white and color photography."

In reply to a question from Darby, Betty said: "You
believe in immortality. Until actual laboratory work is
ready, you have to go on laying the foundations. I want
to chart some kind of course to be followed later scientifically . . . to get over in terms of mechanics the possibility
of the two worlds being the same."

Then came the analogy of the electric fan. One of the
things that makes it seem to us like separate universes,
Betty said, is frequency. When a fan is running fast—that
is, when the blades are passing at high frequency—we
look right through the blades without seeing them. "If
the frequency were different for your human focus, you
could see me. As it is, you look through me." One of the
sitters suggested that it must feel like looking at fish in an
aquarium—that is, considered from the point of view of
the "other side." "As with the fish in the bowl, we can see
them, we inhabit the same universe, but we cannot live
with them." Betty seemed to accept this and responded
with the photography parallel. A black-and-white photograph registers a reality. A color photograph registers the
same reality but gives many more dimensions than the
black and white. "It helped us to understand," White
wrote, "how there might be different appearances of the
same thing." Betty insisted: "If you can discover the frequency, you can reveal my universe. That does not mean
you can inhabit it yet. It would mean you would know I
am inhabiting it." Though only newly arrived, Betty was
able to affirm Myers' concept of levels of consciousness:
"The mode of existence of certain individuals is farther
out into the whole."

Betty next undertook to "bring a picture of the existence in which I now have my being." She began by re-
minding Joan's sitters that there exists much that our
senses cannot detect, but that has been proved to exist by
means of instruments. The difference between the two
states of being, she said, was mainly one of "awareness-
mechanism"—their "instruments," or "senses," are
much more finely tuned than ours. Among Betty's revelations were these: "My touch of you is just as real to me as
ever. We can see you. . . . Your world and mine are the
same, only you are not conscious of mine. I see both. . . .
We are all working hard on people who come over suddenly and don't know what is happening to them." Here
she spoke of the great advantage of having some understanding of the transitional phase and meeting the other
world "all clean and glorious and sure."

"Death is much simpler than birth. Earth is the borning place for the purpose of individualization."

In presenting her picture of the afterworld, Betty was
not left entirely on her own. Frequently she would say "I
don't know. Just a minute, I'll ask." The one she often
asked was the Lady Anne, who had several centuries of
experience to draw upon. "Consciousness is the only reality; mind and matter are only aspects of it." Earth consciousness, she explained, is adapted to a universe in
which there are many structures of mind and matter to
bump into. "You bump up against a wall. You bump
against space—distance obstructs you and you have to
overcome it. You bump against time; you say 'I haven't
time' meaning that the fixed duration of a day or a year is
obstructing you. You bump up against thought; people's
ideas are hindering, obstructing you."

Emmet Finley, commenting later on Betty's report, elaborated his impressions as follows: "There is in our world this thing called electricity. We do not know its essence; all we know is how it behaves in obstruction. In the unobstructed universe the essence is known and dealt with. That's why, when we asked Betty if there were electricity and oxygen and bricks and sticks and stones in her world, she answered, yes. But always she added that she knew and dealt with these things, not in their obstructed aspects as we do, but in their essence."

It is made easier to understand, Finley continued, by recalling that physicists have been telling us for some years that there is no material substance as we have understood the term in the past. There are only aggregates of energy. And, of course, modes of perceiving that energy. "Go into a dark room. You blunder around and see nothing. That's one aspect. Now find the electric switch and flood the room with light. You no longer blunder about; now you see furnishings and decorations, colors and shapes. That's another aspect. Yet both aspects are of the same room. And this is the room you were in all the time."

Stewart had the final word: "We know, without a question, that your world, which has forgotten the importance of immortality and the wisdom of recognizing the reality of the oneness of consciousness, is going to recover that knowledge." This, White concluded, meant faith in the immortality of the individual, and the extension of outlook that faith implies.

I am impelled to return once more to Ruth Finley, with whom I began this chapter. This time Ruth— "Joan"—was speaking from the beyond, to one of my sitters, Dr. Sherwood Eddy. This time she was speaking not about the great reaches of creation, but of common, earthly things. "I heard you at Oberlin years ago," she told Dr. Eddy. "You were introduced by Dr. Leacock and you almost persuaded me to become a student volunteer missionary. But I broke the spell by going to work for the Cleveland *News!*"

VII

Experience and Explanation

THE PRECEDING CHAPTERS have been largely concerned with people who, though of our own century and perhaps with dates overlapping our own, are not at this moment our contemporaries on the earth plane. This is by design. The whole story of the life beyond death is one of two modes of existence. This is most convincingly told by those who have experienced the entire sequence: our physical world, the transition experience we call "death," and the life beyond it. Persons seeking immediate contemporary testimony will find an ample supply in my other writings. The emphasis of the present work is not upon this world, but upon the one known in physical existence as the future one.

Nevertheless, our witness, to be complete, should bring us up to the immediate present and into the range of living authorities. A few often-repeated questions still remain dangling—hence this chapter of "loose ends," with questions and answers from right now and from recent generations. For example: "What is the difference between hypnotic trance and mediumistic trance?"

In a famous lecture given at Swarthmore College in 1951, Professor C. J. Ducasse of Brown University considered the various modern explanations of what happens in trance mediumship, examined them thoroughly, and gave the conclusions he had reached after many years of careful study. The Ducasse lecture, which has become a kind of classic in its field, discusses a number of the difficulties in evaluating what happens, or can happen, during trance. These possibilities include intentional fraud, unintentional or unconscious fraud, play-acting under suggestibility by one of the medium's secondary personalities, actual communications from persons who once occupied earth-plane bodies, and a combination of these factors. In the course of his lecture Ducasse gave a close-up account of the thoroughness exercised by psychical researchers during their investigations.

The case singled out for special attention was that of Mrs. Lenore Piper. Skeptics sometimes assert that mediums, directly or through collaborators, gather advance information about the families and relatives of people expected to appear, by appointment, for a séance. In the Piper case, both Mrs. Piper and her husband were watched for many weeks by detectives, to find out whether they had been going around asking about relatives and family histories of people expected to come for sittings. "Nothing in the slightest degree suspicious was ever found." Besides, sitters were always introduced by assumed names. Sometimes they were not even in the room when the medium went into trance; when they entered, they took a position where the medium could not have seen them even if her eyes had been open. On her trip to England she stayed in lodgings selected by the investigators and was kept under surveillance by them. All her mail was opened and read.

Yet her mediumship continued to produce conclusive evidence of survival. Much of the information she gave out could not have been gathered even by the most expert of detectives given unlimited time. There was no possible way, the investigators concluded after having the medium, her associates, and her manner of life under close observation for many years, that she could have collected such information about so many sitters and their departed friends, by known and natural means. "There is in her case no escape from the fact," Ducasse concluded, "that this information had some para-normal source."

Next, he considered the possibility of another explanation often set forth: that the medium had extraordinary powers of extracting, by telepathic means, information, feelings, plans, intents, and experiences stored in the memories and unconscious minds of living people anywhere on earth. But to explain what actually happens, one would have to postulate even more. Besides obtaining the informational content, one would have to suppose that the disassociated secondary personalities of the medium would be able to impersonate, "whether automatically or deliberately but often with notable verisimilitude," the dead friend of the sitter.

Here it was necessary to consider some of the things that have happened in ordinary hypnotic trance (Ducasse was careful to point out that hypnotic trance is not the same as mediumistic trance, though the two states may easily be confused) . "The hypnotized subject enacts with surprising convincingness the role of any character, which, as a result of suggestion, he imagines himself to be." On numerous occasions, fake names and names of fictional characters have been suggested to persons under hypnotic trance, and vivid interpretations have been given back. Since people in trance have been found to have "extensive clairvoyant and telepathic powers," any truly scientific analysis of mediumistic results would have to take into account *all* possibilities being mixed together in a single session or séance and needing to be disentangled by a trained analytical mind.

This, incidentally, is what is meant by the degree of "purity" or "quality" of the work of a given medium; a high percentage of clearly evidential communication from discarnate personalities is said to be "pure" or "of high quality." In the particular case of the Piper mediumship, such trained investigators as Professor Hyslop, after long study, concluded that any other conclusion than that he had been talking with his dead relatives in person would "involve me in too many improbabilities."

Ducasse said that a close study of the transcripts renders the impersonation hypothesis in some cases implausible. "Some of the keenest-minded and best informed persons," said Ducasse, "who approached these phenomena with complete initial skepticism and studied them over many years in the most acutely critical spirit, eventually came to the conclusion that, in some cases at least, only the survival hypothesis remained plausible."

Hyslop thought that the general reluctance of scientists to accept the survival hypothesis was due mainly to fear. There were no theoretical difficulties in the way of complete acceptance of life after death. It would, however, require a whole new start for science. "The tremendous consequences—philosophical, moral, religious and political—that must follow anything like scientific proof of a future life make it necessary that we should not be fooled in so important a matter as this." The contention that survival is impossible has been maintained only by a tenacious clinging to "a certain metaphysical assumption which is quite arbitrary and which automatically begs the whole question."

Ducasse sums up: "It can be shown that the supposition that individual conscious life continues in some form after death is something that can be said to have been really established either by the natural sciences or by philosophy. There is empirical evidence that the individual's mind does survive death and that it occasionally manages to communicate with the living."

Another question is often asked: "What is the effect of prayer, now and in the afterlife?"

One of the most powerful mediums of the late nineteenth century was that of a British clergyman, W. Stainton Moses, who ministered to a parish in the Isle of Man. Moses' mediumship began when he was asked to "look into" spiritualism by a physician friend. Moses, at that time convinced that spiritualism was trickery, began attending séances—and developed one of the most powerful mediumships of his day. Voices of spirit communicators were sometimes heard independently. There were levitations of the medium and of furniture, objects were brought from other rooms through closed doors, and direct writing was produced independently of any living human hand.

Moses is best known for the religious and inspirational books he wrote by automatic writing. His communicators were a group of twenty-two discarnate personalities directed by a chief who always signed himself "Imperator." Through Imperator and his associates, and the advice and instructions they imparted, Moses came to abandon the orthodox religious views absorbed during training for the ministry, in favor of concepts the "other side" imparted to him by his automatic writings. An example is the matter of the efficacy of prayer. While his communicators agreed that prayer was necessary for spiritual safety and growth, their explication of the channels through which prayers are routed was not the conventional one.

"You would pray more did you know how rich a spiritual blessing prayer brings. Your learned sages have discussed much of the value of prayer, and have wandered in a maze of opinion, befogged and ignorant of the real issue. They do not know—how should they? —of the angel messengers who hover around ready to help the spirit that cries to its god. . . . Frequently it is the unspoken petition which is not granted that is the cause of richest blessings to the praying soul. The very cry of the burdened spirit shot forth into the void —a cry wrung out of bitter sorrow—is an unknown relief . . . many times to grant his request would be to do him grievous harm. He has asked ignorantly, petulantly, foolishly: and his prayer is unheeded in its request: but it has availed to place his spirit in communion with an intelligence which is waiting an opportunity of approach, and which can minister to him strength and consolation in his necessity. It were well if men would more strive to live a life of prayer. Not the morbid life of devotions falsely so called, which consists in neglecting duty and in spending the precious hours of the probation life in morbid self-anatomy, in developing unhealthy self-scrutiny, or in

forced and unreal supplication. Prayer to be real must
be the heart cry, spontaneous and impulsive, to friends
who hover near. The fancy of a prayer to the ear of an
ever-present God who is willing to alter unalterable
laws in response to a capricious request has done much
to discredit the idea of prayer altogether. Prayer—the
spontaneous cry of the soul to its God through the
friends who, it knows, are near, and are ever ready to
catch up the unuttered petition and bear it upwards
and ever upwards 'til it reach a power that can respond—this is no matter of formal preparation. It
consists not in any act of outward show. It is not necessarily syllabled in utterance: far less is it trammeled
by conventional form, or bound up in stereotyped
phraseology. True prayer is the ready voice of spirit
communing with spirit.

Are sudden and violent death transitions always more
difficult than peaceful ones?

An unusually vivid description of the violent death
transition came in 1917 to an automatic writer who signs
himself W.T.P. from an "other-side" communicator who
gave his name as Thomas Dowding:

Physical death is nothing. There is really no cause
for fear. Some of my pals grieved for me. When I
"went west" they thought I was dead for good. This
is what happened. I have a perfectly clear memory of
the whole incident. I was waiting at the corner of a
traverse to go on guard. It was a fine evening. I had
no special intimation of danger, until I heard the
whiz of a shell. There was an explosion somewhere
behind me. I crouched down involuntarily, but it was
too late. Something struck, hard, hard, hard against
my neck. . . . I fell and as I did so, without passing

through any apparent interval of unconsciousness, I found myself outside myself! You see I am telling my story simply; you will find it easier to understand. You will learn to know what a small incident this dying is . . . five seconds later I was standing outside my body helping two of my pals to carry my body down the trench toward a dressing station. They thought I was senseless but alive. I did not know whether I had jumped out of my body through shell shock, temporarily or forever. You see what a small thing is death, even violent death of war! . . . my pals need not fear death. Few of them do; nevertheless, there is an underlying dread of possible extinction. I dreaded that; many soldiers do, but they rarely have time to think about such things. . . . My body was hoisted onto the stretcher. I wondered when I should get back into it again. You see, I was so little "dead" that I imagined I was still physically alive. . . . I had begun a new chapter of life. I will tell you what I felt like. It was as if I had been running hard until, hot and breathless, I had thrown my overcoat away. The coat was my body, and if I had not thrown it away I should have been suffocated. . . . My body went to the first dressing station, then to a mortuary. I stayed near it all that night, watching, but without thoughts. . . . I still expected to wake up in my body again. Then I lost consciousness and slept soundly. When I awoke, my body had disappeared! How I hunted and hunted! . . . Soon I ceased hunting for it. Then the shock came! It came without any warning, suddenly. I had been killed by a German shell! I was dead! . . . How does it feel to be "dead"? I simply felt free and light. My being seemed to have expanded. . . . I am still evidently in a body of some sort, but I can tell you very little about it. It has no interest for me. It is convenient, does not ache or tire, seems similar in formation to my old body. There is a subtle difference, but I cannot attempt analysis. . . . I was very lonely. I was conscious of none near me. I was neither in the world of matter nor could I be sure I was in any place at all! I think I fell asleep for the second time . . . at last I awoke. . . . A load has dropped away from me. I think my new faculties are now in working order. I can reason and think and feel and move. . . . I am no longer alone—I have met my dear brother who came out here three years ago and has now come to welcome me. William could not get near me for a long time, he says. He hoped to reach me in time to avert the shock, but found it impossible. He is working among the newly arrived and has wide experience.

Does the world beyond always seem strange and unnatural to new arrivals?

The American psychic Edward C. Randall, writing in 1917, reports the following vivid account of the afterlife he received through the medium Mrs. Emily S. French:

The most learned scientist among the inhabitants of earth has practically no conception of the properties of matter, the substance that makes up the universe— visible and invisible. I did not when I lived among you, though I made a special study of the subject. That which you see and touch, making up the physical or tangible, is the lowest expression of life force. . . . On my arrival here there was the meeting and greeting of my own who came to welcome me, as naturally as one returning after a long journey in the earth-life would be welcomed. Their bodies were not so dense as when they were inhabitants of earth, but they were like my own. Then I was told that my body and the bodies of all those in that life were actually the identical bodies which we had in earth-life, divested of the flesh covering. I was also told that the condition is a necessary precedent to entering the higher life, and that such bodies during earth-life had continuity and, further, that in leaving the old, I had come into a plane where all was etheric—that is, matter vibrating in perfect accord with my spirit. Everything seemed perfectly natural to sense, sight and touch. The etheric body alone has sensation. My personal appearance was in no way changed except that my body was less dense. My mind was clear, the appearance of age was gone, and I stood a man in the fullness of my mentality. What impressed me most after the meeting with my own was the reality and tangibility of everything and everyone. . . . It has been our aim to explain the law through which life is continued, and so simply to state the facts and explain the conditions that all may understand. All that you see and touch is only the substance used by life in growth . . . by divesting himself of his physical housing, one is said to take on immortality, but in reality he has always been immortal. . . . We communicate with each other by simple thought projection.

"You have spoken mostly of prearranged séance situations. What about reported spontaneous glimpses into the world beyond?"

Dr. Ralph Harlow, a Smith College professor, writing in 1960, asserted his belief that by a very slight change in the range of our ability to perceive vibrations, we could be aware of persons in the world beyond. We are nearly tuned in, and at rare moments, certain rare individuals have the privilege of being almost completely tuned in.

He tells of a time when he and his wife were strolling in the woods on a spring morning near Ballardville, Massachusetts:

From behind us we heard the murmur of muted voices in the distance. I said to Marion, "we have company." Marion nodded and turned to look. We saw nothing, but the voices were coming nearer—at a faster pace than we were walking, and we knew that the strangers would soon overtake us. We then perceived that the sounds were not only behind us but above us, and we looked up. About ten feet above us and slightly to our left, was a floating group of glorious, beautiful creatures glowing with spiritual beauty. We stopped and stared as they passed above us. There were six of them, young beautiful women dressed in flowing white garments and engaged in earnest conversation. If they were aware of our existence they gave no indication of it. Their faces were perfectly clear to us, and one woman, slightly older than the rest, was especially beautiful. Her dark hair was pulled back, and although I cannot say it was bound at the back of her head it appeared to be. She was talking intently to a younger spirit whose back was towards us and who looked up into the face of the woman who was talking. Neither Marion nor I could understand their words although their voices were clearly heard. They seemed to float past us, and their graceful motions seemed natural—as gentle and peaceful as the morning itself. As they passed, their conversation grew fainter until it faded out entirely, and we stood transfixed. We looked at each other, each wondering if the other had also seen. "Come," I said, and led her to a fallen birch. We sat and I said "Now, Marion, what did you see? Tell me exactly in precise detail. And tell me what you heard." She knew my intent—to test my own eyes and ears; to see whether I had been the victim of hallucinations. Her reply was identical in every respect to what my own senses had reported to me. "For those split seconds," she said calmly, "the veil between our world and the spirit world was lifted."

Professor of psychology Elmer T. Gates, writing in 1920, was convinced—as was Dr. Richard Maurice Bucke —that cosmic consciousness, or immortality, could be achieved while the individual is still on the earth plane and in his physical body:

> There is that in the universe which has succeeded; has produced worlds and peopled them with evolving life; in the very fact that evolution has taken place, it shows the triumph of good over evil, the victory of knowledge over ignorance. That which has succeeded is Mind, or consciousness; . . . you and I have inherited that nature, and are possessed by the spirit, meaning and promise of that greatest mystery of existence —consciousness. By means of Mind all possibilities are open to us; and when we study its nature we are studying the nature of the supreme mind and are directly conscious of that which has been eternally ruling in cosmos. Whatever problems are solved by the future will be solved by consciousness, whether these problems relate to the objective or the subjective world.

On the earth plane, says Gates, man's nearest approach to the cosmic consciousness is through his intuition. He quotes Henri Bergson: "Through intuition it is possible to discover the meaning of life, the very nature of existence." The cosmic consciousness must have a nature more fundamental than our own limited individual experience, Gates reasons, and it is from this cosmic consciousness that there wells up into our individual awareness the insights and intuitions that illuminate our understanding. The "priceless possession" within the reach of all is the possibility of realizing immortality through one's own inner consciousness.

The place of sex in the afterworld has often been the subject of query of earth-side people when in séance communication with those who have gone beyond. The answers, though given with great varieties of phrasing, have a certain consistency. Jesus answered that people are neither given nor taken in marriage but are "as angels." "Betty" reported that earth, not the world beyond, was "the borning place." Raymond Lodge said, "Children are not born here." Yet the essence of sexuality somehow continues, apparently. One vivid account of its expression in this farther world was given through the automatic writing of a medium known as Jennifer, to the author Basil King, who has passed it on in these words:

> The sexes continue, sex being part of individuality. They grow nearer together in sympathy, but more diverse in gifts. They are two separate forces of God. They clash radiantly, producing energy and love. The contrasting and harmonizing elements are like flint and steel, and the flame of their spiritual contact is divine passion—the creative force from which not children are born, but power.

"If psychical researchers are so extremely fussy, what kind of material *do* they regard as what they call 'evidential'—that is, as clear proof that the communication was indeed from a person who had once lived on this earth and had died, and nothing else?"

In my other two books, *Nothing So Strange* and *Unknown but Known,* I have compiled some cases from my own mediumship that have passed the most rigorous tests. For now, since this book is about something else and any discussion of evidential material is by way of a digression, I will let the point go by citing a single case that most psychical researchers agree is flawless and without loophole.

On March 19, 1917, Mrs. Hugh Talbot, a widow, had a séance with Mrs. Gladys Leonard, and her control, "Feda." Witnesses were present. This is Mrs. Talbot's account of the sitting:

> Feda gave a very correct description of my husband's personal appearance, and from then on he alone seemed to speak, and a most extraordinary conversation followed. Evidently he was trying by every means in his power to prove to me his identity and to show me it really was himself. As time went on I was forced to believe this was indeed so. All he said, or rather Feda for him, was clear and lucid. Incidents of the past, known only to him and to me were spoken of, belongings trivial in themselves but possessing for him a particular personal interest of which I was aware, were minutely and correctly described, and I was asked if I still had them. Also I was asked repeatedly if I believed it was himself speaking. I was assured that death was really not death at all, that life continued not so very unlike this life and that he did not feel changed at all. . . .
>
> Suddenly Feda began a tiresome description of a book. She said it was leather and dark, and tried to

show me the size. . . . "It is not exactly a book, it is not printed, Feda wouldn't call it a book, it has writing in." It was long before I could connect this description with anything at all, but at last I remembered a red leather notebook of my husband's, which I think he called a log book. . . . I said "Is it a red book?" On this point there was hesitation. They thought possibly it was, though he thought it was darker. Then Feda said "He is not sure it is page 12, it might be 13, it is so long, but he does want you to look and try and find it. It would interest him to know if this extract is there."

I was rather half-hearted in responding to all this, there was so much of it and it sounded purposeless. I remembered the book well, having often looked through it wondering if it was any good keeping it. Besides things to do with ships and my husband's work there were, I remembered, a few notes and verses in it. But the chief reason I was anxious to get off the subject was that I felt sure the book would not be forthcoming. Either I had thrown it away, or it had gone with a lot of other things to a luggage room in the opposite block of flats where it would hardly be possible to get at it. . . . Feda became more and more insistent: "He is not sure of the color, he does not know. There are two books, you will know the one he means by a diagram of languages in the front. . . . Will you look at page 12 or 13? If it is there, it would interest him so much after this conversation. He *does* want you to, he wants you to promise."

After dinner the same evening my niece, who had taken more notice of all this than either my sister or myself, begged me to look for the book at once. . . . I went to the bookshelf, and after some time, right at the back of the top shelf, I found one or two old notebooks belonging to my husband, which I had never felt I cared to open. One, a shabby black leather, corresponded in size to the description given and I absentmindedly opened it, wondering in my mind whether the one I was looking for had been destroyed or only sent away. To my utter astonishment, my eyes fell on the words, "Table of Semitic or Syro-Arabian Languages!" This was the "diagram of languages!"

Mrs. Talbot then turned to page 13 of the notebook, and there, copied in her husband's hand, was the following excerpt from a book called *Post Mortem,* written by an anonymous author and published by Blackwood:

I discovered by certain whispers which it was supposed I was unable to hear and from certain glances of curiosity or commiseration which it was supposed I was unable to see, that I was near death . . . presently my mind began to dwell not only on happiness which was to come, but upon happiness which I was actually enjoying. I saw long-forgotten forms, playmates, school fellows, companions of my youth and of my old age, who one and all smiled upon me. They did not smile with any compassion, that I no longer felt I needed, but with that sort of kindness which is exchanged by people who are equally happy. I saw my mother, father, and sisters, all of whom I had survived. They did not speak, yet they communicated to me their unaltered and unalterable affection. At about the time when they appeared, I made an effort to realize my bodily situation . . . that is, I endeavored to connect my soul with the body which lay on the bed in my house . . . the endeavor failed. I was dead. . . .

VIII

Reflections on My Own Mediumship; Yogananda; A Special Word to the Newly Bereaved

DURING ONE of the eight sittings I conducted in which Ruth ("Joan") Finley spoke through Fletcher from the other world, she made the following statement: "Ford is his own master of ceremonies. He is here with us, on what you call our plane. . . . Sometimes Ford is so much interested in what is being said here that he goes off with his cronies on this side and lets someone else man the station. There are other discarnate personalities who have approximately his energy pattern and can, if given leave, feed impressions to Fletcher."

On hearing this, one of my sitters wanted to know whether I could remember anything about these excursions into the other side, as Ruth Finley could during her mediumistic experiences while she was on the earth plane. I had to answer that I could not. Whatever travels I may have had in these realms are completely sealed off from my conscious recollection. A trance, to me, was a dreamless sleep.

This is not to say that I have not had experiences on the "other side." One of the most vivid experiences of my entire life was, in fact, just such a journey into the higher realms. Some years ago I had an experience that forever lifted this whole matter of survival out of the realm of faith and brought it clearly down to the plane of realism, so far as I am concerned. Though I have told this story before, it bears so specifically on our present context that I must tell it again.

I was critically ill. The doctors said I could not live, but as the good doctors they were, they continued doing what they could. I was in a hospital, and my friends had been told that I could not live through the night. As from a distance, with no feeling except a mild curiosity, I heard a doctor say to a nurse, "Give him the needle, he might as well be comfortable." This, I seemed to sense, was "it," but I was not afraid. I was simply wondering how long it would take to die.

Next, I was floating in the air above my bed. I could see my body but had no interest in it. There was a feeling of peace, a sense that all was well. Now I lapsed into a time-less blank. When I recovered consciousness, I found my-self floating through space, without effort, without any sense that I possessed a body as I had known my body. Yet I was I *myself*.

Now there appeared a green valley with mountains on all sides, illuminated everywhere by a brilliance of light and color impossible to describe. People were coming toward me from all around, people I had known and thought of as "dead." I knew them all. Many I had not thought of for years, but it seemed that everyone I had ever cared about was there to greet me. Recognition was more by personality than by physical attributes. They had changed ages. Some who had passed on in old age were now young, and some who had passed on while children had now matured.

I have often had the experience of traveling to a foreign country, being met by friends and introduced to the local customs and taken to places of interest any visitor to the country would want to see. It was like that now. Never have I been so royally greeted. I was shown all the things they seemed to think I should see. My memory of these places is as clear as my impression of the countries I have visited in this life: The beauty of a sunrise viewed from a peak in the Swiss Alps, the Blue Grotto of Capri, the hot, dusty roads of India are no more powerfully etched in my memory than the spirit world in which I knew myself to be. Time has never dimmed the memory of it. It is as vivid and real as anything I have ever known.

There was one surprise: Some people I would have expected to see here were not present. I asked about them. In the instant of asking a thin transparent film seemed to fall over my eyes. The light grew dimmer, and colors lost their brilliance. I could no longer see those to whom I had been speaking, but through a haze I saw those for whom I had asked. They, too, were real, but as I looked at them, I felt my own body become heavy; earthly thoughts crowded into my mind. It was evident to me that I was being shown a lower sphere. I called to them; they seemed to hear me, but I could not hear a reply. Then it was over. A gentle being who looked like a symbol of eternal youth, but radiated power and wisdom, stood by me. "Don't worry about them," he said. "They can come here whenever they want to if they desire it more than anything else."

Everyone here was busy. They were continually occupied with mysterious errands and seemed to be very happy. Several of those to whom I had been bound by close ties in the past did not seem to be much interested in me. Others I had known only slightly became my companions. I understood that this was right and natural. The law of affinity determined our relationships here.

At some point—I had no awareness of time—I found myself standing before a dazzling white building. Entering, I was told to wait in an enormous anteroom. They said I was to remain here until some sort of disposition had been made of my case. Through wide doors I could glimpse two long tables with people sitting at them and talking—about me. Guiltily I began an inventory of my life. It did not make a pretty picture. The people at the long tables were also reviewing the record, but the things that worried me did not seem to have much interest for them. The conventional sins I was warned about as a child were hardly mentioned. But there was sober concern over such matters as selfishness, egotism, stupidity. The word "dissipation" occurred over and over—not in the usual sense of intemperance but as waste of energies, gifts, and opportunities. On the other side of the scale were some simple, kindly things such as we all do from time to time without thinking them of much consequence. The "judges" were trying to make out the main *trend* of my life. They mentioned my having failed to accomplish "what he *knew* he had to finish."

There was a purpose for me, it seemed, and I had not fulfilled it. There was a plan for my life, and I had misread the blueprint. "They're going to send me back," I thought, and I didn't like it. Never did I discover who these people were. They repeatedly used the word "record"; perhaps the Akashic Record of the ancient mystery schools—the great universal spiritual sound track on which all events are recorded.

When I was told I had to return to my body, I fought having to get back into that beaten, diseased hulk I had left behind in a Coral Gables hospital. I was standing before a door. I knew if I passed through it, I would be back where I had been. I decided I wouldn't go. Like a spoiled child in a tantrum, I pushed my feet against the wall and fought. There was a sudden sense of hurtling through space. I opened my eyes and looked into the face of a nurse. I had been in a coma for more than two weeks.

Several things occurred to me as factors which have inhibited our ability to apprehend the realities of the beta body and of the expanded universe available to it. Perhaps the most formidable is the misconception that our five senses—sight, hearing, taste, smell, and touch—are the only means of knowing that we have. It is obvious, if we would only stop to think, that we have many more senses than these. Nobody has ever seen a person. We see the physical body of the person and some of the kinetic effects it produces, but the person himself is invisible. Our consciousness resides even now in the same beta body it will inhabit in its further journeys. We know people not through the gross five senses but through subtler awarenesses of the beta bodies.

In this sense, speaking from the point of view of the workaday world, we are already invisible and should not be surprised if the actualities of deeply experienced life are not available to our outer eyes and ears. The beta body can be prepared for its further journey beginning here and now. Character is developed not in the act of dying but in the act of living. Spiritual illumination is no more reached in a single step than is physical perfection or intellectual attainment. One cannot convince another of the truth of immortality by intellectual arguments or external evidence. It must be known by that inward awareness which is part of every human psyche. It is that awareness which, as Wordsworth put it, comes as "A sense sublime/Of something far more deeply interfused . . ./A motion and a spirit, that impels/All thinking things, all objects of all thought,/And rolls through all things."

Of all the people I have ever known, the saintly and at the same time urbane Paramahansa Yogananda possessed this sense in the highest degree. On first meeting this extraordinary man, I recognized immediately that I was in the presence of great spiritual stature. Yogananda was not a mere theorizer and preacher of doctrine; through healing, through clairvoyance, through prophecy, and in many other ways, he could demonstrate the truths he taught. Unfortunately, I cannot say that I was ever a disciple of this distinguished guru. When I first met him as a young man, I was in no mood to undertake the disciplines required for such character transformation. He did not hold this against me; a good teacher, he was always patient with me. Unimpressed by my psychic abili-

ties, which he regarded as mere side effects, he calmly
held before his students a constant vision of the higher,
ultimate meanings of creation.

It was largely through Yogananda's influence that I
finally went to India and underwent a brief exposure to
the swamis' methods of spiritual conditioning. The general run of swamis did not greatly impress me. However,
here and there, I could see developing true spiritual
greatness. But I decided it was not for me, at least at that
time. I was too intoxicated by the pleasures of physical
self-indulgence, to say nothing of other and more direct
intoxicants. If all this effort was required to attain a deep
character transformation, I decided, lightheartedly, I
would just have to bounce along through life with whatever character I had. But my admiration for Yogananda
never diminished. He has been one of the great spiritual
lights of my life. Knowing him, seeing his demonstrations, and imbibing his teachings—even when I found
myself unable to follow them—have been an unfailing
inspiration.

To Yogananda, the command of pure consciousness
over all forms of material energies, the oneness of the
divine creative consciousness with the essential self of the
individual human were more than mere doctrinal concepts. They were living realities. The constant and conscious transactions with these forces over a long life had
brought Yogananda experiences which, to the average
"practical" man knowing little about these forces and
their control, seem incredible. Yet they were so often
demonstrated, and given to the world with such a sweet
modesty, that no one who knew him could easily set

aside his perceptions of the various levels of consciousness.

Yogananda's visions carried him into cosmic consciousness, and some of his most penetrating teachings concerning the life beyond death came from this level of awareness. "The tragedy of death is unreal; those who shudder at it are like ignorant actors who die of fright on the stage when nothing more has been fired than a blank cartridge." Once, in meditation, his beta body became fully manifest to him in earth consciousness. "One's values are profoundly changed when he is finally convinced that creation is a vast motion picture; and that not in it, but beyond it, lies his own reality. I sat on my bed in the lotus posture. My room was dimly lit by two shaded lamps. Lifting my gaze, I noticed that the ceiling was dotted with small mustard-colored lights, scintillating and quivering with a radium-like lustre. Myriads of penciled rays, like sheets of rain, gathered into a transparent shaft and poured silently upon me. At once my physical body lost its grossness and became metamorphosed into astral texture. I felt a floating sensation as, barely touching the bed, the weightless body shifted slightly and alternately to left and right."

Yogananda liked to tell the story of Thales of Miletus, the Greek sage who lived six centuries before Christ. Thales taught that there was no difference between life and death. "Why, then," asked a critic, "do you not die?" "Because," answered Thales, "it makes no difference." Yogananda, always an intensely human person, knew perfectly well that, in terms of human emotions, it does make a difference. He himself was overwhelmed by grief

when he lost—to the very "death" he knew to be illusory
—one of his loved ones. On the death of his guru, Sri
Yukteswar, he had instant knowledge of the passing.
Moment-of-death experiences—a vivid awareness of the
passing of someone who is at a distance—are among the
best documented of all psychic phenomena, and so it was
in no sense unusual. Yogananda was on a train when his
old teacher died in a distant city. "There was a sudden
black astral cloud; later a vision of Sri Yukteswar appeared before me. He was sitting, very grave of counte-
nance, with a light on each side. 'Is it all over?' I lifted my
arms beseechingly. He nodded, then slowly vanished."
Sri Yukteswar, Yogananda later learned, had died at
the exact moment of the vision. He had predicted the
time of his own death, gone into meditation as it approached, and left impressed on his physical face an expression of joy.

Yogananda, a Hindu, did not question the resurrec-
tion of Jesus but did question its uniqueness. If the real
self is a mental-spiritual structure of pure consciousness
and if this consciousness can control such lower forms of
energy as physical substance at its own will, then there
was, to Yogananda, nothing remarkable about such a consciousness choosing to reassemble some molecular structures on any occasion when it desired to appear before the
everyday sight of friends still in the earth plane. In this
manner, Sri Yukteswar appeared to Yogananda exactly
as Jesus did to his Disciples.

The event was known also to other distinguished gurus
of India and in the twentieth century. The following was
related to Yogananda by another swami: "Here in Cal-
cutta, at ten o'clock of the morning that followed his cre-

mation, Lahiri Mahasaya appeared before me in living glory." From another disciple of the same guru: "A few days before Lahiri Mahasaya left his body, I received from him a letter that asked me to come to Benares. I could not leave at once. Just as I was preparing to leave, about ten o'clock in the morning, I was overwhelmed with joy to see in my room the shining figure of my guru. 'Why hurry to Benares?' Lahiri Mahasaya said, smiling. 'You shall find me there no longer.' As the import of his words dawned on me, I cried out brokenheartedly, believing that I was seeing him only in a vision. 'Here, touch my flesh,' he said. 'I am living as always.' "

Yogananda had a similar experience following the death of his own guru, Sri Yukteswar. The great teacher appeared in Yogananda's room at the Regent Hotel in Bombay at three o'clock in the afternoon of June 19, 1936—more than three months after his presumed death. Spontaneously, the emotional Yogananda rushed to embrace his old teacher and found his arms around a substantial body. Yogananda exclaimed over this, and Sri Yukteswar explained: "Yes, this is a flesh-and-blood body. To your sight it is physical. From the cosmic atoms I created an entirely new body, exactly like that physical body which was buried."

Sri Yukteswar talked of the worlds beyond death: "Beings with unredeemed earthly karma are not permitted after astral death to go to the high causal sphere of cosmic ideas. They must shuttle between the physical and astral worlds, conscious successively of their physical body and of their astral body. . . ." There were many parallels with Myers' planes of consciousness: "Long-established residents of the beautiful astral universe,

freed forever from all material longings, need return no
more to the gross vibrations of earth. Such beings have
only astral and causal karma to work out. At astral depth
these beings pass to the infinitely finer and more delicate
causal world. Shedding the thought form of the causal
body at the end of a certain span, determined by cosmic
law, these advanced beings are again reborn in a new astral body." After a two-hour talk, Sri Yukteswar said, "I
leave you now, beloved one!" and melted away.

The same guru made an appearance to an old woman
who had lived near his hermitage. Nearly two weeks after
his death, she arrived at the ashram and asked to see her
guru. On being told that he was dead, she reported, un-
believingly: "Impossible! This morning at ten o'clock he
passed in his usual walk before my door. I talked to him
for several minutes in the bright outdoors." Yogananda's
sharp observation and rigorous honesty did not miss reporting that even in so great a soul as Sri Yukteswar, a
very human teacher of very human beings, there existed
the same fear of death, the same animal reluctance to
part from a habitual bodily residence, that attends us all.
When, near his eighty-first birthday, Sri Yukteswar announced that he would soon die, he was, though very
briefly, visibly upset. "For a moment," Yogananda said,
"he trembled like a frightened child." Yogananda then
recalled the words of another great guru: "Attachment to
bodily residence, springing up of its own nature, is present in slight degree even in great saints." Sri Yukteswar
had said the same thing in these words: "A long-caged
bird hesitates to leave its accustomed home when the
door is opened." Sri Yukteswar quickly regained his
poise and remained in blissful peace throughout his

death passage. During his after-death reappearance in the hotel room, the great teacher passed on these reassurances: "Unwilling death, disease and old age are the curse of earth, where man has allowed his consciousness to identify itself almost wholly with a frail physical body requiring constant aid from air, food, and sleep in order to exist at all. The astral world is free from these three dreads." He then spoke of what Betty White had referred to as the Unrestricted Universe: "By quick dematerialization, I now travel instantly by light express . . . wherein did I die?"

After an experience of this kind—one of the uncounted death-door experiences known to every generation and having an amazing similarity of content and structure—one returns to the accounts of the afterlife from other sources with a new conviction. Since I have been reared and trained in the Christian tradition, I naturally think first of the sayings of Jesus. "You shall be with me. . . . I go to prepare a place for you. . . . You in me, I in my father. . . . My Father's house has many mansions. . . . Do not touch me, I have not yet risen . . . Between them is a great gulf fixed." In these and similar sayings I find the whole structure of the afterlife as I knew it during those days when I was out of my body: the astral body, the continuing on the other side with memory and recognition, the various levels of consciousness and development, the kindly and helpful treatment of those newly arrived on the other side, the progress toward the comprehension of and cooperation with the creative principle, the universe, God.

On reviewing the record of man's experience with the "other side" since the beginning of his recorded exist-

The Survival Beliefs of Man
A Condensed Tabular Statement

EPOCH	Astral Body	After-Death Lingering	Memory Survival	Levels or Stages
Stone Age (25,000 B.C.)	X	X	X	
India (From 5000 B.C.)	X		X	
Egypt (c. 2000 B.C.)	X		X	X
Mysteries (c. 1000 B.C.)	X		X	X
Judaism (From 2000 B.C.)	X		X	X
Greek (c. 500 B.C.)	X	X	X	X
Chinese (From 500 B.C.)			X	
Christian (From A.D. 35)	X	X	X	X
Tibetan (From A.D. 1000)	X	X	X	X
Dante 13th century A.D.	X	X	X	X
Swedenborg 18th century	X		X	X
Myers 19th century	X	X	X	X
Hyslop 20th century	X			X
Hodgson 20th century	X		X	
Lodge 20th century	X	X	X	X
James 20th century	X		X	
Betty 20th century	X	X	X	X
Broad (Contemporary)	X		X	
Murphy (Contemporary)	X		X	
Ducasse (Contemporary)	X		X	
Contemporary Demonstrations	X	X	X	X

Earth-like Plane	Light-like Higher Plane	Medium-ship	Helping New-comers	Progress Toward Comprehension of Creative Principle, God
		X		
X				X
X				
X	X	X		
X	X	X		
X		X		
X		X		
X	X	X	X	X
X	X	X	X	X
X	X	X	X	X
X	X	X	X	X
X	X	X	X	X
X		X		
		X		
X	X	X	X	X
		X	X	
X	X	X	X	X
		X		
		X		
		X		
X	X	X	X	X

ence on earth, I am struck by the consistency of all reports as to the general experience of the afterlife and the
overall structure of the afterworld. To be sure, each reporting generation uses its own imagery, idiom, and symbols, and each national or racial group uses its own cultural forms of expression. But the basic thing they are
talking about remains essentially the same. Where Jesus
says "many mansions," the *Tibetan Book of the Dead*
says "The Western Realm Named Happy," "The South-
ern Realm Endowed with Glory," "The Eastern Realm
Called Pre-eminently Happy," "The Central Realm of
the Densely Packed," and "The Primary Clear Light."
Myers mentions "The Seven Stages"; Betty, "Those
farther out beyond"; Raymond, "Those who have been
here longer and know more." It is impossible to read
these firsthand accounts and not develop a conviction
that they all are talking about the same psychic energies
and structures. These forms, I am very sure, constitute
the very nature, plan, purpose, and eventual fulfillment
of the life beyond death—an ever-widening experience of
understanding, brilliance, spiritual power, achievement,
and joy.

The loftiest minds, the most generous hearts, the most
penetrating intelligences, the noblest souls of recorded
history have affirmed the continuance of human life and
charted the way. Shall I, then, be put off by the jaundiced carping of lesser minds and smaller souls? For
nearly half a century my work has been at the disposal of
scientists, and I have personally known a goodly number
of them. It has never been the great ones who have denied the continuance of life. In fact, I doubt that the yap-
ping of lower-echelon scientists is as much responsible for

the prevailing inability to believe what has been clearly demonstrated about survival as the lower-echelon religionists. For too many centuries, too many peanut-minded, sour-souled bigots, and power drivers have sought to dominate their flocks through threats of hell. The joys, freedoms, and opportunities of the unobstructed universe beyond have been all but lost sight of. Fear does not attract; it repels. Fear-of-hell preaching is, I think, as much responsible for our prevailing disbelief as anything else. Who wants to believe in an afterlife if it's something unpleasant?

The length the hellfire preachers, both Protestant and Catholic, will go is almost beyond belief. In a pamphlet I picked up in a Roman Catholic church not long ago I found these words: "Little child, if you go to hell, there will be a devil at your side to strike you. He will go on striking you every minute forever and ever without stopping. The first stroke will make your body as bad as the body of Job, covered from head to foot with sores and ulcers. The second stroke will make your body twice as bad as the body of Job. The third stroke will make your body three times as bad as the body of Job. How, then, will your body be, after the devil has been striking it every moment, for a hundred million years without stopping? Go tomorrow evening at seven o'clock and ask what the child is doing. The devils will come back and say 'The child is burning.' Go in a million years, and ask the same question. The answer is just the same: 'it is burning.' So, if you go forever and ever, you will always get the same answer, 'it is burning in the fire.' "

Protestantism can easily match this one, whopper for whopper. This is from a book of Protestant sermons:

"When you die your soul will be tormented alone. That will be a hell for it. But at the day of judgment your body will join your soul, and then you will have twin hells; your soul sweating drops of blood, and your body suffused with agony. In fire, exactly like that we have on earth, your body will burn forever unconsumed, all your veins roads for the feet of pain to travel on, every nerve a string, on which the devil can forever play his diabolical tune of hell's unutterable lament." Can people regularly exposed to this kind of thing—the sadistic, megalomaniac projections of a sick mind's frustrations and resentments—possibly look forward to an afterlife with anything but dread?

Fortunately, a fair proportion of churchgoers have not been exposed to this kind of psychopathology. If they have only shadowy and fearful notions about the afterlife, there must be some other reason. This can readily be found, I think, in the pattern of the lives we lead— sometimes seem almost forced to lead. The daily grind of earning a living, maintaining a front, and doing necessary chores leaves little energy for the kind of spiritual effort that would result in a constant assurance of an open-ended life that goes on into a glorious infinite. Even a child given kindly and inspired instruction concerning the afterlife quickly notices that his parents are paying little attention to such instruction during the week— they are busy and preoccupied with other things. Only as death approaches, only at the moment of death, only at the shock of bereavement and loss, does it come home crushingly that these things matter.

In the First World War, I lost a brother. I grieved for him. I was a young man then. In later years I lost other loved ones, and I grieved for them. Part of my work as a minister and part of my ministry as a medium have been to deal with people made distraught by grief. I am not unacquainted with grief.

Bereavement is a complex thing. One cannot deal with it simply by assuring the stricken person that all is well with his loved one. Intellectually, he may be well aware of that fact. Belief in a benevolent, glowing new opportunity in the life beyond could be one of the very cornerstones of a person's character, and yet that person could experience a seemingly unendurable grief. One must separate out the other elements of the agony of bereavement before the clear knowledge of the reenergizing nature of the new life can do its healing, restorative work.

Life, as actually lived by us, is very largely a matter of emotional relationships—tugs and pulls, attractions and repulsions—between human beings. In this sense, each of our lives is made up of the lives of others. When one life is seemingly removed from this earth-plane pattern, the whole pattern shakes, and those closest to the one who has "graduated" are most deeply affected. Ties with cosmic and spiritual life and its greater perspectives can ease this pain but not eliminate it. On the earth plane our spiritual bodies are incubating, and our earth bodies have a powerful sway. They have their habits, their appetites, their imprints, their long conditioning in familiar ways. When one of these behavior circuits must be drastically rearranged, the result is unavoidable pain.

When this disruption is severe, it may stir up a whole nest of deeply buried feelings that the bereaved is now forced to contend with. These feelings are so common and so widespread—as well as so intense—that they were among the subjects to which Sigmund Freud gave his pioneering attention. Besides the simple sadness because of loss, Freud sometimes found a complicated network of dejection, loss of interest in real experience, and feelings of being punished or expecting to be punished. He pointed out that just because a person was physically gone did not mean that the person's imprint, deepened perhaps over years, was not still vivid in the mourner's memory. The tension between absence and emotional presence needs to be recognized. "The normal outcome," wrote Freud, "is that deference for reality gains the day." The realities, of course, are spiritual ones. A healthy mind, aided by the understanding and solicitude of friends, gradually finds that earth impressions fade as the truth of the ever-opening continuance of human life takes over. Sometimes, says Freud, it is slow: "Each single one of the memories and hopes which bound the libido to the object is brought up . . . and detachment . . . is accomplished." Though the process may be slow, it is, given faith, sure.

A famous study of acute grief as experienced by survivors of the terrible Cocoanut Grove fire in Boston, by Erich Lindemann, was published in *The American Journal of Psychiatry* in 1944. Lindemann, discovering a common pattern in grief reactions, substantiated Freud's findings and went a step beyond. It is not only attachments of love and affection that affect the mourner, but also bondage of hostility or resentment. In both cases the old patterns of life involving the one who has gone beyond must be relived and adjusted, step by step. Gradually, the adjustment is made, sometimes leaving the mourner a greater, deeper, finer person than he was before his loss. The best that friends and counselors can do during such a time is to help create a friendly and favorable emotional attitude so that the inner resources of the mourner himself can restore him.

There are, of course, individual reactions which do not follow the common pattern. A person may try to bury his sense of loss in an outburst of frenzied activity. Or he may do the opposite and apparently show no grief at all —until some later explosion. But when the bereaved is willing to face the full pain of his loss, recognize it for what it is and call on his reserve strength to reorganize his life, he regains his zest for living. It is at such times that a clear knowledge of this world as only the first of a sequence of worlds, each more highly and finely energized than the one before it, can do its transforming work.

And then, of course, there is the matter of confronting the reality of one's own approaching death. Here, too, I have had some experience. My life has been checkered with close calls—horrendous accidents, sharp bouts with dangerous diseases, crises brought on by my own addictive folly. But these are mere narrow escapes; once over, one tends to shrug them off.

I have undertaken this book with the fairly certain knowledge that it will be my last. I have had so many heart attacks, strung out over so many years, that one would have to be abnormally dense to miss the point that the final one cannot be far off. I wish I were a better patient. I wish I did not have to be so grumpy and hard to deal with when I am sick. I positively, almost angrily, dislike being sick. Dying? Dying is another matter. I almost did it once before and found it one of the great, memorable, ecstatic experiences of my life. I can see no reason why the real thing should be less joyous than the trial run. I know that great opportunities await us where we are all going. I hope, when the time comes, I will have completed that earth task for which I believe my life in the earth sphere was fashioned: to use whatever special talents were given me, through no merit of mine, to remove for all time the fear of the death passage from earth minds, and to raise the curtain a little bit for a glimpse of the glory beyond.

THE IMPACT OF ARTHUR FORD AS PHENOMENON:
An Epilogue

The Impact of Arthur Ford
as Phenomenon: An Epilogue

ARTHUR FORD was, and is, my friend. Our friendship is based on mutual liking, common interest, and mutual respect; it has never interfered with each of us doing his own thing. During the years of our earth-side friendship, Arthur was the world's most renowned trance medium, and I was a professional observer and reporter of events.

Our friendship was colored by our professional predilections. Arthur was always interested in the psychic and spiritual development of my life. I could not help being interested in Arthur, not only as a friend, but as a phenomenon. His gift, though not unique, was rare. Its impact on the public credulity was an extraordinary thing to observe and, I think, full of significance for the future development of our species.

Arthur Ford was under the observation of science—and of an extremely sophisticated, advanced science—longer than any other medium in history. The last American medium of Ford's stature, Daniel Dunglas

Home, was also under continuous observation for nearly forty years. The phenomena he produced were extremely well attested. They are too remote from us in time, however, to have much weight in the age of materialistic skepticism from which we are only now emerging. Home performed during the third quarter of the nineteenth century. It is easy for the skeptic to say, and be believed by an audience predisposed to being skeptical anyway, that the observation techniques of those days were primitive and the evidence therefore is questionable. Ford has been another matter. He was subjected to every test a highly developed science of psychical research could devise and passed them all. As a result, he has had an enormous impact on public thinking.

Arthur, a typical child of his age, had an almost childlike awe of men of science. I used to guy him about it. "You'll find just as many boneheads among scientists," I told him, out of many years of campus associations, "as you will among other classes of people." He would waggle his head and recount the scientists he had known, and still knew, who were solid supporters and amiable companions. He had an astonishing range of acquaintance. In it were a number of scientists, and among these, I knew from having met them, were some highly competent and most agreeable gentlemen.

The best scientists are men who look carefully at evidence that comes to them—that is what makes them the best. As a class, however, scientists are most disappointing. They tend to be narrow, specialty-bound, overprideful of their limited set spiel, and contemptuous of anything outside their range. This kind of mind has arrived at dogma, and dogma finds no need for evidence. These minds, rather than the great ones, set the general tone of the science of our day, and I have found it exasperating. Arthur, however, never lost patience. He seemed to have faith that if he continued to smother them with evidence, someday they would learn. He was often treated rudely, sometimes openly insulted, by men with scientific credentials. He persevered, deeply convinced that his particular mission in life was to continue the production of evidence whose value would someday be recognized.

During the past decade there has been a distinct change in the climate of public esteem for science. We have already noted the philosophical observation that every great cultural movement eventually becomes its opposite. Has this point now arrived in the history of science? Christianity, which began with sacrificial brotherly love and became a sadistic inquisition, is often cited as an example. At the time of the Inquisition, the scientist Galileo stood as a courageous example of progressive clear thinking and openmindedness. Today dogma has come to science, and a great many scientists feel no need to study evidence that tends to refute their established dogma.

This has led to some catastrophic blunders, and these catastrophes have not escaped public notice. Some of our leading scientists have repeatedly given public assurance that the fallout from the early atomic test explosions was perfectly harmless. Time produced contrary testimony; heavy concentrations of radioactivity developed in milk from milk sheds all along the path of atmospheric drift from the sites of the explosions. The famous "baby-tooth survey" revealed unusual concentrations of radioactivity in the teeth of babies along the path of the fallout drift. DDT was offered by science as the ideal solution to the problem of insect pests: It was miraculously effective and, "science" said, harmless to other forms of life. The wholesale and worldwide destruction caused by this chemical proved them wrong. Unsavory alliances began to be observed between science and other interests. We have developed military men who demand a weapon capable of exterminating the entire human race, and there has never been a lack of scientific men to oblige them. Scientists disagree, one group claiming that a quantity of genocidal poison dumped into the ocean will do the ocean no harm, another group denying it. Frequently, science has allied itself with venal advertising. Big Business discovered it could bribe "science" to do or say about anything it demanded, and Big Military made the same discovery.

The inevitable result was another demonstration of the historical law. What had begun as openminded truth with Galileo had become, in high places, arrogant, bigoted, dogmatic.

This, of course, is not intended as a sweeping indictment. Some of our most accomplished natural scientists are even more deeply concerned about the waywardness of science than those of us who now see public judgment being pronounced. For the fact is that people do not trust science as blindly as they did ten years ago. For a number of years all you had to do is say "scientists have found" to command immediate and respectful attention. There was a time when "the church authorities have ruled" commanded the same instant and respectful hearing. Both groups have now lost the power to command such automatic and unquestioned credulity—and for the same reason: Their statements have been found too often to be untrue. Science is no longer taken as the final word. People who have said all along that modern science had taken a wrong turn years ago are beginning to have a better hearing. This is particularly true of those who have insisted that metaphysics is more fundamental than physics, that the primary structure of the universe is conscious and mental rather than mechanical and physical. The teachings of the Edgar Cayces and the Arthur Fords are getting a better hearing.

Numerous straws point the direction of the wind. Astrology is a field Arthur never had much to do with, but it will serve as an example of an area which had been generally regarded as irrational, occult, and unscientific. It has not been so many years since one of our leading national magazines published an article, quoting scientific authority, asserting that astrology was a "gigantic fraud." Today astrology is enjoying an unprecedented boom.

There could be no better illustration of the progress of an insight from openminded truth to closeminded dogma than the history of astrology. In the beginning, the craft was quite scientific. It had been observed over thousands of years that babies born into the mildness of spring and summer had a better chance of survival than babies born into the hostile rigors of autumn and winter. Since the arrival of the seasons varied with latitude and longitude, keen and thoughtful observers concluded, quite sensibly, that both the place of one's birth and its date had something to do with how one got along in life. Even if the fall or winter babies survived, the struggles of the first months of life were seen to have left their lasting mark.

From these and many similar observations there grew a complex system of behavioral theory, some of it making a good deal of sense.

Then the apparently inevitable historic rule set in: What had been knowledge became dogma; dogma became arrogant; arrogance led to blunders and then to loss of the general respect. Mediumship was running a similar course at about the same time. The Old Testament prophets rail with impartial vigor against "wizards [astrologers] and mediums." The knowledge-to-dogma-to-discredit sequence runs something like this: mediumship, astrology, religion, philosophy, science. Each in turn made a promising beginning and discredited itself. Yet each contained some truth. What will be the next step of man in his long quest of comprehension of the universe he is part of? Might it not be a return of a kind of openminded inquiry that could distinguish between dead dogma and living truth? Might it not reclaim those bits of truth from the long past that mankind so desperately needs in its survival crisis? Then might it not add to these treasures whatever bits of truth we may be able to find in our own time?

Science—the lively, inquiring arm, not the dead academic branch—has recently come upon evidence that astrology may not be the "gigantic fraud" so many learned men had supposed it to be. Astrology's major claim—that human lives are affected by extraterrestrial forces—has been abundantly justified. In 1947 E. R. Dewey and E. F. Dakin compiled the facts about business cycles from such centers of learning and research as Harvard, Princeton, Yale, and Columbia. Variations in solar radiation, it had been shown, correspond with ups and downs in business activity. Changes in ozone levels, atmospheric electricity, and ultraviolet radiation, "due presumably to the sun but perhaps also to the whole solar system," do influence the behavior of man. "Our social sciences have tended to forget, in the bravura of modern times," wrote Professor E. Huntington of Yale in 1938, "a fact that to the ancients was quite clear: man is a child of the sun." We are reminded of this by our simple act of getting up, going to bed and planning vacations. That we are also children of the moon is borne in upon us by the tides, by the widely documented upsurges of mental disturbances and crime around full moon, by menstrual cycles.

We are also influenced by the outer planets. In 1951, J. H. Nelson, a scientist employed by the Radio Corporation of America, published a scientific paper on the predictability of the magnetic storms that play hob with the world's radio traffic. These storms, he said, were related to the positions of the planets around the sun. The solar system is like a great electrical generator: "the sun is the armature, the planets are the magnets."

Here he was following the lead of the great seventeenth-century "father of modern astronomy" Johannes Kepler. When the planets are distributed at angles of 90° or 180°, Nelson found, magnetic storms are probable. Distributions of 60° or 120° mean storm-free radio weather. Remarkably enough, the angles 90° and 180° ("square" and "opposition") have since ancient times been regarded by astrologers as unfavorable, while 60° and 120° ("sextile" and "trine") have been pronounced beneficent. Magnetic turbulence is not the only kind of storm in which science and astrology meet. Kepler had worked out a complete system of weather astrology. Later astronomers inclined to discount this as a mere quirk of Kepler's, but recent findings have confirmed the old master. The first twentieth-century scientific presentation of weather astrology was made to the American Meteorological Society in 1964 by George McCormack, a name famous among astrologers. McCormack, who runs his own weather bureau and sells its service to firms needing dependable forecasts (airlines, fruit ranchers etc.), again followed Kepler's lead in asserting that weather follows laws similar to those governing magnetic storms— and earthquakes. McCormack has correctly predicted the recent major earthquakes, beginning with the 1933 Long Beach disaster and including the Alaskan quake of 1964.

Scientists had long assumed that creatures following tidal, solar, and seasonal rhythms learned about cyclic changes through the usual sensory signals—weather, water movements, sunshine. Professor F. A. Brown of Northwestern University and the Marine Biological Laboratory at Woods Hole, Massachusetts, began ten years ago to observe living creatures in sealed quarters where environmental factors such as temperature, illumination, humidity, and biometric pressure never changed. To Brown's astonishment, the confined creatures maintained their rhythm without interruption. Potato buds followed the seasons as faithfully as potatoes living in a normal environment. Somehow, though in perpetual artificial twilight, they always knew the position of the sun. Oysters, when moved a thousand miles inland from their native beaches, timed their opening and closing according to the tidal rhythms that would have prevailed at that precise inland point had the sea extended that far. Somehow they knew where the moon and sun were at every moment. Just how they achieved this knowledge is one of the unsolved mysteries of organic life. It has been definitely established that living creatures do react, in ways still not understood, to influences from outside the earth. Some of these forces operate, in Brown's words, "at energy levels so low that we have hitherto considered the living organisms completely oblivious to them. There are still unknown temporal and spatial, subtle and pervasive forces influencing behavior of living things."

Cleve Backster, by demonstrating with the polygraph that plants react emotionally to events of their environment—particularly to human intentions—has shown that we live in a living and sensitive environment, not an inert and dead one. He has also shown that the force which communicates emotional intent—still unmeasured and still unidentified by science—easily penetrates any known physical obstacle, including walls of lead and concrete. Again, "subtle and pervasive forces influence the behavior of living things."

Thus, belatedly and reluctantly, science has come to admit the existence of subtle and unknown forces. Could this possibly be the beginning of wisdom? Electricity was once such an unknown force; its essential nature is still unknown. Its behavior, however, has been so carefully observed and charted that man can cooperate with it and utilize it for his own purposes. Should not *all* the subtle and unknown forces at work among us be the legitimate subjects of careful, methodical, scientific inquiry?

The parallels with the work of Arthur Ford are obvious. For forty years he produced substantial and consistent evidence that man's ancient belief that his personality survives biological death with memory, recognition, and capacity for growth is not a religious hypothesis but a scientific fact. Many scientists took advantage of his generous and always available cooperation to observe for themselves. These came away convinced and endorsed the statement: Man survives death. But because the forces by which physically deceased persons communicate are "subtle and unknown," the main body of science has been slow to take its cue for further inquiries.

This may well prove to be the rock on which dogmatic science will founder. Ford demonstrated the phenomenon of communication from those presumed dead; he demonstrated on four continents over four decades, sometimes, through television, to millions of witnesses. Historically, denial of valid evidence has never affected the validity of the evidence; rather, it has rendered obsolete both the denial and those who deny. If positivist philosophy and materialistic science continue on their course of denial without investigation, they will join the other categories of obsolete and discarded beliefs. No one is suggesting, of course, that the dogmatic astrology and dogmatic spiritualism be given any more credence than dogmatic denial. What is suggested is that those demonstrated forces which provided the original impetus toward belief in survival be given their due attention, quite apart from any dogma which may have grown up around them. The case of astrology is instructive. Ten years ago astrology was a "gigantic fraud." Today our most reputable scientists are affirming the basic phenomena on which the *original* astrologers based their claims. Is not a similar revival of the study of survival evidence long overdue? We are providing government research grants for a dizzying variety of practical and impractical manipulations of physical things. Some of them are quite trivial. Is there anything more important, to all citizens, than a further and more detailed knowledge of the ultimate psychic life toward which we all are moving?

A beginning has been made in the investigations of reincarnation made by the University of Virginia's famous professor of psychology Ian Stevenson and by the several psychiatrists who have employed memory regression in hypnosis to uncover recollections of another existence. After careful investigations of reported cases of reincarnation in children, Professor Stevenson reported that on the basis of the evidence, the traditional hypothesis of reincarnation seems more appropriate than any alternative.

Sometimes a case of this kind is so startling it breaks into print and comes to the attention of millions. Only recently there was such a case: An eight-year-old girl in India began to speak in most urgent terms of her immediate need to "see her husband." Her parents' assurances that she was only eight years old and had no husband were of no avail. The distraught child was taken to a psychiatrist who advised the parents to follow the child's suggestions and see what happened. At the girl's behest, a taxi was summoned; the driver took her to an address she gave him. There without hesitation she went to a particular apartment and found a man. She gave him explicit directions on where to find things he had been looking for and gave him other information that seemed greatly to relieve his mind. He thanked the child, and she left, now completely restored to her normal self. The man was a widower whose wife had died just before the time the child began to demand to "see her husband."

In every generation for more than 10,000 years, man has been given overpowering evidence that his personality will survive death. The authenticity of this evidence becomes more convincing the more carefully it is observed. There is no rational reason why a general acceptance of the fact of survival should be delayed any longer.

What a marvelous change in our attitudes, our plans, our ambitions, our behavior, and our general welfare would come about if we believed this tremendous fact and translated our beliefs into action! It would certainly mean a rebirth of science, which now stands stymied at the ball of its own disbelief. Once we turn our full powers of methodical inquiry toward those forces which science can now only dismiss lamely as "subtle and unknown," a new and world-transcending existence will have opened for all of us. We will come to know as much about the world beyond death as we now know about the world beyond the horizon. The dread of death will vanish, the threat of death will have lost its power, and all who depend upon this threat for their authority will be displaced. A new psychology will emerge with a new motivation. No longer will man be driven by a frenzy to take to himself as much of this world's goods and experience as possible before death blows the whistle on his gain. Our motivations will begin to be oriented toward life rather than toward death. We will be splendidly reborn.

I am not sure that the entire blame for our failure to begin to realize such a vista can be laid entirely at the door of a reactionary element within the scientific establishment. There is reason to think that another factor may be involved—a predominant personality type that may be designated the All-American Hard Guy. Our little boys are trained to this pattern just to the extent that they can and will endure it. You have to learn to play the game, and the game is usually body contact and tough. As soon as they are old enough for basic training, our young men are taught the karate chop, the killing kick, and the death stomp. The only respectable place to be is at the top, and the man at the top is always a Hard Guy. He is practical, meaning that he deals only in tangibles. Anything intangible, unless it can immediately produce tangibles, is immediately brushed aside by the Hard Guy at the top, because it is probably fuzzy, dreamy, and impractical and because the Hard Guy is so practical. There is currently a saying in business circles that "nice guys don't make president of the bank."

Such ruthless practicality, history has patiently been telling us for a number of centuries now, does not work very well. Other nations, of course, have their Hard Guys, each convinced that his own national brand of hardness is the hardest of all. The ultimate tragedy of the practical man is that he is impractical. Because his calculations leave out of account certain "subtle and unknown forces," they carry him to decisions that lead to his own destruction.

This is daily becoming less of an academic assertion and more of a visible fact. Practical men are on the very brink of destroying, by the poisons they release through their extremely practical activities, the very environment that sustains them. Unless they become practical enough to curb themselves in time, practical men and women will produce, in the next thirty years, more children than

were born in the preceding million years. Such overpro-
duction would certainly mean the end of human life as
we have known it and possibly the end of all human life
in its physical form. To bring on worldwide famines, immeasurable suffering, and probable extinction does not
seem very practical. The All-American Hard Guy is obsolete. So are his brothers round the world. The time is
nigh for men and women who have the vision to think,
feel, plan, and live in the ultimate extensions of human
and cosmic insight.

I confidently expect a new and universal world
religion to emerge—and soon. In the beginning it will
have two branches, one terrestrial and physical the other
cosmic and psychical. These two branches are emerging
quite separately, but will presently begin to see that they
are of one root.

Their beginnings can already be seen. The terrestrial
and physical branch is beginning to make itself known
under the name of ecology. At no time since the beginning of the industrial-technological revolution have so
many human beings been concerned about the relation
of man to his total environment. Water, air, and fertile
earth, industrial man is beginning to relearn, are the
stuff from which his earthbody is made. Unless they are
available in sufficient quantity and in pure form his earth
body will perish. With this knowledge he is approaching
his environment with a new respect and recapturing
some of the knowledge of it he had once known but had
forgotten. He is rediscovering that earth is not inert but
conscious, with a consciousness comparable in some respects of his own. It reacts to him. A mutual dependency
exists.

He is at last beginning to comprehend the meaning of the Biblical injunction that he "has dominion" over the creatures. The Cosmic Creative Principle itself has shared the earth with him, taken him into full partnership, made him earth's administrator. Both his opportunity and his responsibility are bounded only by the dimensions of earth itself. What he makes of it and of himself is much more his own doing than he has ever before realized. Physically, ecologists like Professor Brown are beginning to realize that the environment—the *physical* environment—affecting man extends far beyond earth and moon and their gravitational fields. Man, in a strictly physical sense, is cosmic.

At the same time that man's ecological consciousness—his awareness of local and outer space—has been expanding, so has his depth-psychological experience—his exploration of inner space. Once this psychic realm is opened, its relationship to the physical realm becomes clear. Man and the living creatures of earth are seen as products of the cosmic—or, if a religious word be permitted, divine—imagination. The power of the creative imagination over physical things becomes apparent. All —physical *and* psychical—is seen to be one. The Great Project of Creation is seen to be evolution—not just of physical shapes, color, activities, and forms, which in themselves are exciting to the limit of our senses to bear —but of consciousness, of awareness, of the ability to comprehend.

As this comprehension establishes its beachhead and spreads from there, the outlines of the Many Mansions begin to be seen—world upon world of exquisitely structured psychic soul space to be explored, understood

and mastered. A few such explorations have already
begun on a methodical basis. Prominent among these are
the researches with various mind-expanding drugs by Dr.
Walter Pahnke and his associates, under government
grants, at the Maryland State Psychiatric Research Center. A few of these drugs may be compared to nitroglyc-
erin: deadly when used without understanding by
amateurs, life-stretching when used with the guidance
and insights of medical and psychiatric science.

The Eastern techniques of deep meditation, of which
Arthur's old teacher Yogananda was a master, have led
many, in both East and West, to expanded immediate
awareness, a clear perception of higher levels of comprehension, and even to cosmic consciousness. These two
movements—the broadened awareness of the physical
universe through ecology and the deepened comprehension of the psyche by meditation—are not static but
growing. As the cults of scientism, positivism, and strict
materialism have revealed their limitations, the human
spirit reaches out for dimensions in which it may find its
full and ultimate stature. For a certainty, these outward
and inward reachings will become aware of their oneness,
and for a certainty, this will constitute the new world
religion.

Since this new religion will have its seat within the individual human consciousness, there probably will not
be very many administrative jobs, hence little occasion
for ranks, prerogatives, and titles. There will be no build-
ing-fund drives, because there will be no buildings.
There will be no bazaars, no bingo games, and little
ritual. Men and women will recognize one another as fel-

low beings. The world of the hereafter and the world of now will be seen as a continuum.

There will be no saints, but men like Arthur Ford will be seen as rugged pioneers of the new comprehension. He gave himself unswervingly to his task as he saw it: the persistent espousal of the truth it was given to him to know, in the face of every opposition and discouragement, to the end that men and women might understand themselves and their cosmos more completely.

It is as well for Arthur, I am certain he agrees, that in the new dispensation there should be no saints. Arthur, as he saw at once when he encountered the genuinely saintly Yogananda, did not have the makings of a saint. At his best, he was master of droll humor, featuring the wry quip. If he had not been a great trance medium, he would have been a great deadpan comedian. At his worst, he was well-nigh impossible to get along with. He was a very human Arthur, and I loved him and still love him, with the affection of those who understand and tolerate one another's foibles. Of such, I am convinced, is the kingdom of heaven.

He will be heard from, of course. He has already made known his safe arrival on the other side and the beginning of his period of rest, adjustment, and acclimatization. Not many weeks after his death a message, received by a "board" medium in Gainesville, Florida, was forwarded to me by a council member of Spiritual Frontiers Fellowship (SFF): "Ford here . . . my message is this: life after death is a reality . . . explore SFF . . . read chapter 7, page 70 *Unknown but Known* . . . your son Terry has the book . . . SFF has many answers, contact them. I am tired, must rest."

And what of Fletcher, that sturdy co-worker of Arthur's, that peppery master of ceremonies whose shrewd adjudication made his personality almost as well known to the psychically aware public as Arthur's own? In a series of séances held during the six months before Arthur's death, Fletcher gave his own answer to this question. Arthur's death was anticipated, by those, both on this side and in the beyond, who knew the state of his physical health. Fletcher explained that in his sphere, as in ours, people work in groups. One has associates and superiors. One works in some extent under direction. One has responsibilities to one's group and is to some extent under orders. Fletcher's assigned job, he said, was to stand by Arthur and be his master of ceremonies until Arthur graduated from the earth plane. Once Arthur passed over, Fletcher was to be freed for further explorations in the higher realms of consciousness.

From this we may take it as a certainty that Fletcher will never be heard from on earth again. He regarded the final period of his employment as Arthur's control as a burden. He was anxious to get on, to explore those glowing, enticing lands just over his visible horizon.

Arthur's "Gainesville Message"? The following is the significant quote from Chapter Seven of the paperback edition of Ford's book *Unknown but Known*; the chapter opens on page 70, under the chapter title "An End to the Fear of Death," with this quote just beneath the chapter heading:

A general emancipation from the searing grip of this most fearsome of all dreads would free tremendous human energies for the creative tasks of life. And there is no *rational* reason for delaying any longer a general enjoyment of this immeasurable benefit. A hundred years of careful research has established the essential fact of survival to the satisfaction of all who approach the evidence with a free mind. Three thousand years of demonstration by prophets, saints and heroes has suggested the capacity for expanded living that results when a human being casts aside his fear of death. There is no longer, I repeat, any rational reason to consider biological death a final end, or to fear it.

Guilford   JEROME ELLISON
Summer, 1971.

INDEX